Cinemas of Hertf...

The Embassy Waltham Cross in 1937. The building survives but this wonderful lighting scheme does not.

Cinemas of Hertfordshire

ALLEN EYLES

WITH KEITH SKONE

HERTFORDSHIRE PUBLICATIONS

an imprint of the
University of Hertfordshire Press

First published in 1985 by Hertfordshire Publications and Premier Bioscope

This edition published in Great Britain in 2002 by
Hertfordshire Publications
an imprint of the
University of Hertfordshire Press
Learning and Information Services
University of Hertfordshire
College Lane
Hatfield,
Hertfordshire AL10 9AB

ISBN 0 9542189 0 6

British Library Cataloguing in Publication Data
A catalogue record for this book is available from the British Library

Design by Geoff Green, Cambridge CB4 5RA
Cover design by John Robertshaw, Harpenden AL5 2JB
Printed in Great Britain by Antony Rowe Ltd., Chippenham SN14 6LH

ACKNOWLEDGEMENTS

The following generously assisted in the compilation of the first (1985) edition of this book (besides others indicated in the captions as the source of pictures):

Shelagh Head, the Hertfordshire Local Studies Librarian, who extended a warm welcome on our visits to Hertford; John Squires, Kevin Wheelan, David Jones, Martin Tapsell, Percy Birtchnell, and Paul Francis, who generously and promptly provided illustrations and/or information; Eric Brandreth, who showered us with so much of his own private research into Harpenden cinemas; Philip Plumb, whose valuable help solved many of the problems of researching Buntingford; Tony Moss of the Cinema Organ Society, who supplied notes on organ history; Arthur Jones, Hon. Editor, Hertfordshire Publications, for his interest and support ; Martin Ayres, Hugh Corrance, John Foskett and Margaret Shepherd, who entrusted us with irreplaceable illustrations; and Elizabeth St Hill Davies of the Stevenage Museum, Grant Longman of the Bushey Museum Trust, Mr. Johnson of Watford Central Library, the First Garden City Museum (Letchworth), Mary Gilbert, Wally Wilson, Veronica Hitchcock, and Gordon Coombes.

In writing this revised edition, the author is particularly grateful to:

Al Alvarez, Vice President of Operations, Cine-UK, for his help in visiting and illustrating the Cineworld multiplexes at Bishop's Stortford and Stevenage; *Borehamwood and Elstree Times* (Rod Brewster, Charles Whitney); Eric Brandreth of Harpenden, for again loaning illustrations; Dorothy Cleal for permitting extensive quotation from her vivid reminiscences about the Regal Standon and Sawbridgeworth Cinema published in *Hertfordshire Countryside*; the Dacorum Heritage Trust (Matt Wheeler, curator); Elstree and Borehamwood Museum; Stephen Herbert, for his help regarding early film shows in Barnet; Ian Johnson, old university friend from Loughton, Essex, who kindly chauffeured the author on two whirlwind trips across the border to help update the book; Tony Rogers, for his information, illustrations and tour around Hemel Hempstead; Victor Rose; *The Royston Crow* (John Ball); Frank Snart; Lynette Warren, for her help on the ground in St Albans; and Alan Willmott.

After reminiscences were invited through letters in the local press, the author and publisher were delighted to hear from Evelyn Day, C. T. Duff, Eileen George, Jack Graham, Norman Hacker, Mrs Betty Jenkins, Mrs M. Jeram, Betty Miles, Patricia Nicholls, Mrs Anne V. S. Ramsden, and Ronald Wright – many of whom are quoted in the text, as are some further ex-Hertfordshire cinemagoers contacted via an appeal in the Cinema Theatre Association *Bulletin* and other means.

Our information and illustrations have been culled from many sources over many years but, of course, our research relies heavily on cinema advertising in the local press. For some buildings we have found many photographs; for others, nothing. We hope the appearance of this book will encourage readers to unearth more old photographs, which we would be delighted to hear about.

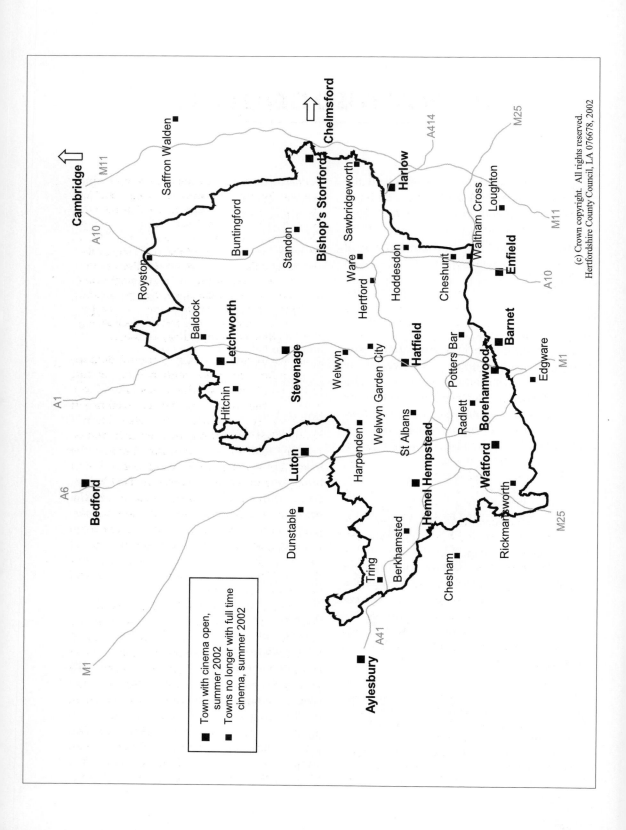

Cambridge ⇧

M11

A10

Saffron Walden ■

Chelmsford ⇧

Buntingford ■

Standon ■

Bishop's Stortford ■
Sawbridgeworth ■

Harlow ■

A414

M25

Loughton ■

Waltham Cross ■

Enfield ■

A10

M11

Royston ■

Ware ■
Hertford ■
Hoddesdon ■
Cheshunt ■

Baldock ■

Letchworth ■

Welwyn ■
Welwyn Garden City ■

Hatfield ■

Potters Bar ■

Barnet ■

Edgware ■

M1

A1

Hitchin ■

Stevenage ■

Radlett ■

Borehamwood ■

A6

Bedford ■

Luton ■

Harpenden ■

St Albans ■

Watford ■

Rickmansworth ■

M25

M1

Dunstable ■

Hemel Hempstead ■

Berkhamsted ■

Chesham ■

Tring ■

A41

Aylesbury ■

Town with cinema open, summer 2002 ■

Towns no longer with full time cinema, summer 2002 ■

INTRODUCTION

During the celebrations of the centenary of cinema in 1996, a 'Cinema 100' plaque was placed in the balcony foyer of the Odeon cinema at Barnet where it remains on view, referring to the town as "The modern home of moving pictures", as pioneered there in 1895–96 by Birt Acres and Robert W. Paul.

As the twentieth century approached, various inventors were working towards recording and projecting images in a way that would give an illusion of movement. Some early experiments took place in Barnet, then fully part of Hertfordshire and not a London Borough.

The first public exhibition of films took place in France on 28 December 1895, in the basement of a Parisian café. The show consisted of a series of shorts made by Louis and Auguste Lumière, using their Cinématographe. A selection of the Lumières' work was then brought to London and shown to paying audiences in the Great Hall of the Polytechnic Institution in Upper Regent Street from 21 February 1896 onwards. This is generally accepted as inaugurating the first public exhibition of films in Britain.

A film historian, Richard Brown, has unearthed a report of an earlier semi-public demonstration of moving pictures being projected on a screen in this country on 10 January 1896. The following small item appeared on an inside page of *The Barnet Press* dated 18 January 1896:

A PHOTOGRAPHIC EXHIBITION – On Friday, the 10th inst., Mr Birt Acres, of Hadley, kindly gave the members and friends of the Lyonsdown Photographic Society a private exhibition of a new photographic invention, a further development of the kinetiscope introduced by Mr Edison. In this apparatus pictures viewed through an optical apparatus are seen in rapid motion. Mr Acres has invented an apparatus for taking pictures on an endless band at the rate from 30 to 50 a second. Among the most successful of his pictures are the "Derby race," "Skirt dancing," and pictures of the ceremony of the opening of the Kiel Canal. He has also been to Berlin and taken pictures of grand royal functions. His new apparatus shows these pictures on a lantern screen, and thus one can see the Derby – the moving horses and the gesticulating crowd – without a dusty journey to Epsom.

This was, of course, a single, one-off demonstration for a specialist audience in contrast to the Lumière show which was offered at a price to the public as an entertainment attraction (the Lumières had also demonstrated their invention, to a French photographic convention months before the December opening). Birt Acres' presentation took place in Barnet because he lived locally and had made films in the area during the previous year in association with another pioneer, Robert W. Paul. The Lyonsdown Photographic Society seems to have met at the Assembly Rooms in Lytton Road, New Barnet. These later became a cinema and were rebuilt as the Regal.

The Lumière show in London was so successful that it was booked into a leading music hall, the Empire in Leicester Square, from 9 March 1896, to become one of the top items on the bill for the next eighteen months. The Empire's rival in Leicester Square, the Alhambra, booked R. W. Paul's British system, the Theatrograph (later Animatograph), from 25 March 1896. The other leading West End variety house, the Palace in Cambridge Circus, adopted the American Biograph from late March 1897 where it remained until 1902.

The film programmes in all these venues were regularly changed.

The new marvel of "animated pictures" spread around the world and into Hertfordshire. Some of R. W. Paul's films were exhibited in a hired hall in Watford in March 1897. Typically, the show included news items such as the Derby and a royal wedding. More "animated photos" were presented in Bushey's village hall on 12 October 1897.

In towns everywhere, programmes of short films continued to be presented in live theatres, by showmen hiring halls and by visiting fairs. When the Hackney Empire in north London opened as a music hall in December 1901, a film projection box was incorporated into the design. But the first purpose-built cinemas were the travelling ones that formed part of fairs, being erected at each temporary showground.

As time passed and audiences still flocked to see moving pictures, from circa 1908 businessmen gained the confidence to take over premises and convert them into full-time cinemas. Shops, railway arches and meeting halls were all adapted for the purpose. Seating was often on benches for little more than a hundred people and shows lasted less than an hour. The conditions under which films were seen often left much to be desired. The highly inflammable film stock was usually projected from within the auditorium and audiences were crammed in the dark with poor ventilation. Lavatories were rarely provided.

Licensing came into effect in January 1910 to ensure better safety standards, requiring a separate projection box and more than one exit in case of fire. The regulations encouraged the construction of purpose-built cinemas with seating on raked or stepped floors to give better sightlines. A new cinema might advertise that its projection booth was "out of sight" and that it could offer "rock steady pictures with no flicker". Many had separate entrances down a side passage for the cheaper seats nearest the screen: this avoided disturbance to the patrons seated further back as well as

saving them from the odours associated with the "great unwashed" – "a very real problem to the public entertainer," noted the 1912 book *How To Run A Picture Theatre*. Attendants used hand sprays between and during performances to provide a sweet scent.

Around this time, the cinema suffered competition from newly built roller-skating rinks but, unlike moving pctures, this proved to be a passing fad and most of the rinks were converted into cinemas. The Super (later Carlton) cinema at Watford was a belated example of this.

This was also the period when censorship first became an issue, with local councils and watch committees objecting to the content of certain films. The industry decided to pre-empt this worrying development by self-regulation, creating and financing the British Board of Film Censors (the last word now amended to Classification). Besides making cuts to completed films, the Board also certified films as 'A' for being more suitable for adults and 'U' as suitable for children. This still allowed local authorities to over-ride the BBFC and lift or impose a ban or change a certificate within their area of jurisdiction.

The purpose-built cinemas of this period generally had elaborate frontages with pay-boxes open to the street and minimal foyer space. The auditoria were usually long halls with straight parallel sides and barrel-vaulted ceilings. Often the side walls had landscape paintings in panels between the pilasters connecting with the ornately decorated ribs across the ceiling. Pianists or small orchestras were engaged to accompany the silent films while many cinemas employed an effects artist to provide sound effects such as galloping horses, rolling waves on the seashore or the shutting of a door. With much smaller overheads than the music hall, cinemas were able to charge very low prices and attract whole families.

From as early as 1908, numerous companies began building chains of cinemas in the more populous towns and suburbs. Hertfordshire did not attract their attention.

Provincial Cinematograph Theatres opened Picture Houses in Dublin, Edinburgh, Manchester, Birmingham, Glasgow and Leicester in 1910. PCT offered continuous performances, then almost unknown, and sought expensive city centre locations, providing a standard of luxury and elegance designed to attract the 'carriage trade' – affluent middle and upper class patrons who would not have stooped to enter the average early picture house. These and other cinemas offered restaurants, cloakrooms and even lounges for reading and for writing letters.

In Hertfordshire, not all early cinemas were one-off local enterprises. Film-making pioneer Arthur Melbourne-Cooper, who had opened the Alpha St Albans in 1908 as an adjunct to his studios, followed this with the Palace Letchworth the following year. (Like the Alpha, the Gem at Borehamwood was another cinema linked to one of the early film production companies in Hertfordshire.)

The advent of the longer feature-length film around 1914 encouraged larger cinemas with better facilities, although major productions were initially presented as special events and often shown in theatres with separate performances at high prices.

World War One

The First World War brought a virtual halt to new cinema construction until the early 1920s but, by that time, some provision for full-time cinema had been made in virtually every Hertfordshire town. Going to the pictures had become a firm part of the local leisure scene.

None of Hertfordshire's early cinemas are still operating. Some were very shortlived. Three of them – the Regent (previously Alpha) St Albans, Bishop's Stortford Cinema and the Royston Cinema – were destroyed by fires in the late 1920s or early 1930s – in at least two cases *not* by the film catching alight in the projectors (as the cinemas were closed at the time) but probably by an unextinguished cigarette in one instance and by faulty wiring in the other. All three were replaced by larger cinemas. Other picture houses such as the Baldock Cinema and Gaiety Tring were made redundant by newer, better cinemas.

But most of the early cinemas carried on

Early Hertfordshire cinemas

1908 St Albans Alpha	Barnet Cinema Palace
1909 Watford Kinetic Picture Palace	1913 Hoddesdon Cinema
Letchworth Palace	Harpenden White Palace
Hemel Hempstead Electric	Royston Cinema
Watford Conservative Club Annexe	Baldock Cinema
1910 Hertford People's Electric	Hitchin Playhouse
Hertford Premier	Waltham Cross Electric Palace
1911 Hitchin Picturedrome	Watford Empire
Berkhamsted Gem	Cheshunt Cinema
Watford Cinema Palace	Buntingford Picturedrome
Ware Picture Hall	Watford Central Hall
1912 St Albans Cinema	1914 Stevenage Cinema
Bishop's Stortford Cinema	Sawbridgeworth Cinema
Bishop's Stortford Empire	Hertford Castle
Rickmansworth Electric	Borehamwood Gem
Watford Electric Coliseum	1916 Tring Empire
Berkhamsted Picture Playhouse	Tring Gem
Tring Gem	1917 Berkhamsted Court
Hemel Hempstead Princess	

until forced to close by declining audiences from the 1950s onwards. The last to surrender was the Empire Watford in 1996 as a result of multiplex competition but by then it had been changed out of all recognition both externally and internally in attempts to disguise its age and keep up with the times. The building still stands – as do a few others also completely transformed. Some rare examples of early purpose-built cinemas elsewhere that were not drastically altered and that have been restored and still show films are the Duke of York's at Brighton, Sussex (1910), Brixton Pavilion in south London (1911, now Ritzy) and the Electric Palace at Harwich, Essex (1911).

The film business had its opponents. It was investigated by the National Council of Public Morals. Reporting in 1917, its Commission of Inquiry calculated that there were 1,076 million attendances per year in Great Britain, representing an average of one visit per fortnight per head of the population. There were approximately 4,500 cinemas, with seats at any one time for one in thirty-seven of the population. The most serious charges levelled against the cinema were an increase in juvenile crime and indecent conduct among the audience. It was suggested that children were influenced by crime on the screen to steal the money for admission, they spread diseases like ringworm and were subject to molestation in the darkness. However, it was conceded in favour of the cinema that it countered the attraction of the public house.

In 1920 attendances nationally surged to their highest level yet. The first British super cinemas, inspired by American examples, arrived in 1921, including the Regent Brighton, the Capitol Cardiff and Rivoli at Whitechapel in London. These were soon followed by such vast picture palaces as the Piccadilly Manchester, Majestic Leeds and Pavilion at Shepherds Bush, west London.

In Hertfordshire, the Grand Cinema Palace at St Albans, opened in 1922, was an elaborate cinema for its time, seating 1,400, although not in a central position. Seven years later, the Plaza Watford was the first super cinema to appear in Hertfordshire with 2,060 seats, the greatest number of seats in a single auditorium of any cinema in the county. It boasted a café, an orchestra pit and an organ, an almost essential feature of a major cinema until the end of the 1930s.

The cinema-building boom

The 1930s was the great decade for the construction of new cinemas in Britain. Cries of "saturation", "surfeit" and "over-building" were commonplace as existing cinema owners attempted to block newcomers, almost always in vain, when they sought planning permission and provisional licence approval. Many older cinemas were extensively modernised or re-built but most were relegated to an inferior position as newer, larger buildings opened up in direct opposition that, because of their size and (often) membership of a large circuit, were able to take over first-run bookings of the best new films.

A consortium of builder John Ray, architect Edgar Simmons and others was behind a series of 1930s cinema schemes in Hertfordshire,

---

New Hertfordshire cinemas of the 1920s

1921 Watford Bohemian	1925 Barnet Hippodrome
Watford Super	1926 Hemel Hempstead Aero
1922 St Albans Grand Cinema Palace	1927 Rickmansworth Picture House
1924 Letchworth Rendezvous	1928 Welwyn Garden City Theatre
Welwyn Garden City Kinema	1929 Watford Plaza
Hemel Hempstead Aero	Radlett Cinema

New Hertfordshire cinemas of the 1930s

1930 Hoddesdon Pavilion	1936 Rickmansworth Odeon
1931 Bishops Stortford Regent	Elstree Studio
St Albans Capitol	Letchworth Broadway
1932 Hitchin Hermitage	Tring Regal
1933 Harpenden Regent	1937 Watford Gaumont
Hertford County	Waltham Cross Embassy
Buntingford Cinema	North Watford Odeon
Royston Priory	1938 Berkhamsted Rex
1934 Potters Bar (Middlesex) Ritz	Welwyn Pavilion
1935 Stevenage Astonia	East Barnet Dominion
Standon Gem	Baldock Astonia
Barnet Odeon	1939 Hitchin Regal
Hatfield Regent	
Harpenden Austral	

most of which showed a marked similarity of style: the Hermitage Hitchin, County Hertford, Odeon Barnet, Dominion Barnet and, without Simmons (who had died), the Regal Hitchin.

From 1927 onwards, new national chains had appeared: both Gaumont and ABC aggressively expanded by building new cinemas and taking over existing ones. The Odeon circuit was a late starter, opening its first cinemas in 1933, but it grew rapidly under the direction of the entrepreneurial genius Oscar Deutsch. All three took a mild interest in Hertfordshire which was not as a whole densely populated enough to greatly interest them.

The ABC group leased from opening the Ritz Potters Bar (when it was part of Middlesex) but soon dropped it as a rare misjudgement. In 1935 the Odeon chain took over the John Ray/Edgar Simmons cinema being built at Barnet. But it was the concentration of population around Watford that most interested these circuits. In 1936 Odeon opened a new cinema in Rickmansworth, near Watford, and took over the Plaza in Watford town centre and renamed it; then in the following year it acquired a cinema under construction in North Watford and opened that as an Odeon as well. A large Gaumont cinema made a debut in the centre of Watford in 1937.

Although Odeon was celebrated for its

house style of streamlined exteriors clad in buff faience, its Hertfordshire properties all had a more restrained look in brick (a cinema planned for the centre of Watford would have been more characteristic, but taking over the Plaza was cheaper and reduced competition).

The company that made the most of the opportunities offered by Hertfordshire was Shipman and King (S&K) which concentrated on taking over and building cinemas in the affluent smaller country towns of the Home Counties, usually becoming the sole cinema operator, often with two outlets to discourage further competition. With nine of its thirty-nine cinemas in Hertfordshire, S&K had the largest number of properties of any company operating in the county. A well-run, very profitable circuit, it operated to high standards and appealed to middle-class audiences. The company first bought the original Hoddesdon Cinema in the mid-1920s and replaced it with their new, larger, better located Pavilion in 1930. In Berkhamsted, S&K acquired the Court in 1930 and completely modernised it in 1934. Then S&K opened a new cinema there in 1938, the Rex, while retaining the Court. Similarly in 1931, the circuit took over the Palace at Waltham Cross, refurbished it and renamed it the Regent, then built the new Embassy across the road in 1937. In 1936, the

Welwyn Garden City Theatre was acquired and substantially altered. In 1937 the recently opened Studio at Borehamwood was taken over. The following year, the Castle and County at Hertford were added to the circuit, the former being extensively modernised.

The cinemas built by S&K in the 1930s were very modern in style and among the best designed in this country. Many of them featured striking interior decoration by the firm of Mollo and Egan (who also worked on the Odeon North Watford).

Other circuits operating in Hertfordshire in the 1930s included Southan Morris's SM Super Cinemas (renamed SM Associated Cinemas in 1948) which was centred on Liverpool but actually started with the Luxor Hemel Hempstead. The D. J. James circuit acquired two important cinemas in St Albans, the Capitol and Grand Palace, as well as the Regent Hatfield; it was taken over in 1937 by General Cinema Finance (GCF), a company in which J. Arthur Rank was a major investor.

Lou Morris was an entrepreneur who took an interest in Hertfordshire, promoting the Capitol St Albans and the cinemas that became the Gaumont in Watford and the Odeon at North Watford. Well known for selling his schemes at a profit, he disposed of the St Albans property soon after opening and the last two before they were even completed. Local operators survived in small towns like Cheshunt and Ware which did not interest the expanding circuits. Noel Ayres built the Astonia cinemas at Stevenage and Baldock.

Mentioned in the coverage of particular towns are several schemes for cinemas that never materialised, but these were usually in places where other cinemas existed or other new ones did open instead. However, it is worth mentioning here that Bushey was targeted for two cinemas although it never did gain one. A scheme was developed for the site of "Purbeck" at Vale Road and London Road with a "lay-out plan" being submitted by architect John W. Green circa May 1936. Also Grant Longman, writing on behalf of the Bushey

Museum Trust in June 1985, reported that the property called "Ye Corner" in Aldenham Road (near the junction with Chalk Hill) had an entrance which was designed to lead into a cinema. The cinema extension was never built and the entrance hall then led to the kiosk of a tattoo artist.

There was considerable opposition to cinemas opening on Sundays, caused mostly by the threat to church attendances but also by the unsuitable nature of the films that were sometimes programmed where it was allowed. Under the Sunday Entertainments Act of 1932, electors were polled in each district where Sunday opening had not been previously established to determine whether or not it should be permitted – unless the matter could be decided at a public meeting without 100 or more people objecting to the outcome. There was usually enough opposition from religious groups to ensure that a poll took place. The result was not a foregone conclusion. In polls held in Hertfordshire in 1938, Rickmansworth came out heavily in favour of Sunday opening, Cheshunt voted narrowly in favour and Hemel Hempstead rejected it by a substantial margin. Sunday opening of English cinemas did not become standard until the late 1950s: even then, one cinema in Bishop's Stortford did not open on Sundays until 1966 because of the religious beliefs of its owners.

The 1930s was also the era when children's Saturday morning pictures took hold. Although the motive was, of course, to wean children into the cinema-going habit at an early age, many cinema operators were careful to ensure that these shows had some uplifting aspects... encouraging good citizenship, road safety and the helping of others.

It is often maintained that cinema-going was primarily a working-class pleasure. There were certainly more cinemas, with lower prices, in densely populated industrial areas, and some in the 'fleapit' category that served a low-income clientèle from the immediate neighbourhood. The size of the working class, allied to its greater need to escape from dire living conditions, made it the greatest constituent of the cinema audience. But it is worth recalling that there was a social stratification based on price at the better cinemas. The best seats in the house, in the front of the balcony or the back of a single-floor auditorium, cost two or three times as much as those closest to the screen and therefore were normally occupied by a different class of patron. Large cinemas had as many as five different seat prices. Invariably, it was the cheapest seats that sold out first (often because they consisted of only a few rows), leaving patrons to decide between queueing until someone left or paying a higher price.

World War Two

When war was declared in September 1939, cinemas and other places of public entertainment were closed for a week as a safety precaution until it was realised that people needed them as a refuge – both literally and as an escape from reality when bombs eventually rained from the sky. Although messages would be flashed on the screen warning of imminent air raids, most cinema-goers preferred to stay put, realising that they were safer in a massive, well-constructed building than out on the street or in their own homes. The only cinema in Hertfordshire that was badly damaged by enemy action was the Castle at Hertford which was closed for more than two years until it could be patched up sufficiently to resume business.

During the war years, the major ABC and Odeon circuits added to their representation in Hertfordshire: ABC gained the Regal Tring as part of a small circuit take-over and Odeon, now led by J. Arthur Rank, took over GCF and with it the Regent Hatfield and both the Capitol and Grand Palace at St Albans in a consolidation of the film chief's interests. SM Super Cinemas added the Princess Hemel Hempstead, Picture House Rickmansworth and the Plaza (ex-Coliseum) and Regal Watford. A new small circuit called London

The manager and assembled youngsters raise their arms to celebrate the opening of an Odeon National Club for Saturday morning pictures for children at the Grand Palace St. Albans in summer 1943. (Courtesy of St. Albans Museums. © Reserved.)

and Provincial took over the Publix Stevenage, Regal Standon and Radlett Cinema.

Helped by a shortage of alternative entertainments, picture-going boomed in the war years, except when areas were subjected to intense bombing (as during the London Blitz) or to evacuation and restricted access. In Hertfordshire, cinemas at Sawbridgeworth and Tring benefitted from servicemen being stationed nearby. In 1941, attendances nationally rose by an amazing 30 per cent over the preceding year and then continued to climb to an all-time peak of 1,635 million admissions in 1946. After this, the figures fell year by year but it was not until 1957 that they declined to pre-war levels of under 1,000 million.

The Second World War put a freeze on cinema construction and it was not until 1955 that building restrictions were relaxed to enable cinemas only half-completed to be finished, and those severely damaged by bombing to be reconstructed. It then became possible to build completely new cinemas and the post-war New Towns with their rapidly expanding populations were prime targets with Odeons being opened at Hemel Hempstead and Harlow in 1960, the latter in Essex but drawing much of its audience from Hertfordshire.

Extended runs of films were confined to the London West End and, on occasion, other major city-centre cinemas. There were one week pre-release presentations at seaside resorts in the holiday season, concurrent with the West End. Films went on general release, beginning with the London suburbs. There had been a simple North London and South London split but, in order to reduce the number of prints in wartime, the suburbs were split up into three regions: North and West, North and East, and South. Barnet and Watford were included in the first week of North and West and showed films before anywhere else in Hertfordshire. Each programme played from Monday for six days, with Sunday (when part of the takings went to charity) being devoted to revivals (which often did excellent business) until the mid-1950s when it became the opening day for new releases (although this later shifted to the current Friday).

Normally, there was no question of a film being held for a second week as another cinema would need the print for its already advertised run. The weekly change of programme was also favoured because it encouraged regular attendance at the same cinema, and many patrons did take the same seat virtually every week, almost regardless of what was showing.

It was customary for two feature-length films to be shown with a newsreel and trailers, making up an approximately three hour show (so that there was only one evening performance). Occasionally, long, spectacular productions played with a "full supporting programme" of shorts and cartoons rather than a supporting feature. After touring the London area, prints played the rest of the country, taking as much as six months to filter down to the really small cinemas in places like Sawbridgeworth and Buntingford. Older, smaller cinemas in Watford that were not part

of a major circuit survived by showing films that had not obtained a circuit release and were usually of limited appeal; these cinemas also revived the most attractive films that had played the major circuits.

In the early 1950s, Hollywood attempted to combat black-and-white television by making more films in colour, and by turning to 3-D and to wide screen systems. Hollywood films also adopted more daring subject matter than was permissible on American television, such as abortion *(Detective Story)* and murder by contract *(Murder Inc.)*, which qualified for the British Board of Film Censors' newly-introduced 'X'-certificate (banning those under sixteen from attending). In Hertfordshire, the Quaker owners of the Regent Bishop's Stortford, besides remaining closed on Sundays, refused on principle to show X-certificate films. But, as described in this book, the same cinema under new management screened a banned Japanese horror film under a special Hertfordshire 'X'-certificate.

In Britain, the slow decline in attendances almost halted in 1954. This was the year in which CinemaScope was introduced by the Hollywood studio, 20th Century-Fox, and the new wide screen shape undoubtedly made a strong initial impression on audiences used to the old 1.33:1 ratio, but within a few years it was taken for granted. Some cinemas baulked at the conversion costs (especially those with the problem of a narrow proscenium arch) and this consideration seems to have brought about the closure of the Plaza (ex-Coliseum) Watford. Fox wanted local cinemas to show films for longer than the traditional one week and also to install stereophonic sound. Both these demands were resisted by the major circuits and Fox supplied its films to other chains that were happy to comply, like Essoldo (a Newcastle concern which had taken over SM Associated). The Essoldos at East Barnet and Watford became part of the so-called Fox or fourth circuit. Only occasional films like *The King And I* actually played more than a week.

The mid-1950s saw the end of the heyday

of cinema-going. Some reminiscences in this book bring out the flavour of that period: when cinemas were a place for children to be amused at Saturday morning pictures, for teenagers to meet up and for couples to go courting (at a time when young people lived at home until they married) and for families to attend as a group. It was a time of three-hour continuous shows when going to the cinema occupied a whole evening (or afternoon), when the programme included one of the five main newsreels (Pathe, Gaumont, British Movietone, British Paramount or Universal) that supplemented the radio and the news-papers with a visual treatment of current events, when queues (especially for the cheaper seats) were commonplace, when cinemas were full of smoke, when youngsters would ask strangers to take them in to 'A'-certificate films they were not legally allowed to see on their own, and when occasionally a young girl might receive unwelcome attention from a man in the darkness.

But above all, it was a time when the cinema meant entertainment on a grand scale, low-cost escapism from the worries of everyday life.

The big decline

Between 1956 and 1960 British cinema attendances more than halved, from 1,101 million to 501. During this period, over 1,000 cinemas shut down, including thirteen in Hertfordshire. These closures in themselves reduced admissions, as not all patrons switched to other cinemas, and also made cinema-going seem unfashionable as they caused newspaper headlines and the unwanted buildings often became derelict eyesores. Undoubtedly, the essential reason for the cinema's decline was the rising standard of living in the home. Whereas some patrons in the 1930s had never stepped on carpet until they went into a super cinema, in the postwar period levels of comfort in the home often outstripped that of cinemas. And, while there had been radio and the

gramophone for home entertainment, now there was television.

BBC Television gained a major boost from the 1953 Coronation of Queen Elizabeth II as half the population clustered around the nation's television sets to watch it as it happened (in black-and-white, of course, enabling a Technicolor documentary, *A Queen is Crowned*, to become the year's biggest box-office attraction in cinemas).

It was the arrival of ITV, region by region, that particularly hurt cinemas as the contractors made more of an effort to appeal to a mass audience than the BBC had done, and also greatly increased the number of still attractive old films that could be seen on the box.

Another highly significant problem faced by cinemas was the decline in the number of new major Hollywood features. Cinemas were struggling to find enough attractive new features to show — many re-issues and feeble programmes went out just to fill the screens. Independent cinemas without access to one of the circuit releases had even less to choose from and the survivors turned increasingly to 'exploitation' features that would appeal to the teenagers and young adults who now made up the bulk of the audience: cheap horror and science-fiction pictures, rock 'n' roll films, nudist features, sexy continental offerings and other sensational fare. Sex or 'adult' films became staple fare at secondary cinemas in Harpenden and Stevenage but failed to bring lasting box-office salvation. Unruly and sometimes violent behaviour by youngsters, especially on Sundays, affected even the bigger cinemas: it began to deter older patrons and gave some cinemas a bad image. Price increases, too, made a visit to the pictures less affordable.

The wider audience lost the habit of attending cinemas regularly and flocked in large numbers only to a few hit films each year, including the Walt Disney holiday releases, leaving other programmes to do mediocre or dire business. Ancillary sales (ice-creams, soft drinks) became increasingly important, as did the revenue from screen advertising. Larger cinemas such as the Gaumont Watford also developed evenings of live shows with pop stars.

In 1958, the product shortage was finally addressed. Fox began to wind down its separate release by giving half its output to Rank's Odeon and Gaumont circuits after a gap of five years. Then Rank regrouped its best outlets from both chains into a new weekly 'Rank release'. Its other cinemas, which included the Gaumonts at Barnet and St Albans, formed the nucleus of a new and misnamed 'National release', weakened by having fewer, mostly inferior, cinemas and by Rank's declaration that it would close many of the outlets when suitable buyers were found. Both the Barnet Gaumont and North Watford Odeon were put up for sale while they were still operating and bought for other uses.

In the past, cinemas had closed down because they were losing too much money. Now cinemas went to be converted to other, potentially more profitable, uses: initially, to become dance halls or bowling alleys, then increasingly to become bingo clubs as the 'eyes down' routine proved to have an enduring appeal. Along with timber yards, cinemas provided the cheapest sites for supermarkets, office blocks, car parks and the like.

Bingo was introduced on a part-time basis from the early 1960s at some cinemas, then often completely replaced films. The Gaumont Watford experimented with Sunday afternoon bingo sessions, the Astoria Ware on that same afternoon and two full evenings. Other cinemas which gave over several nights of the week to bingo were the Curzon Hatfield and the Odeon Hemel Hempstead. Cinemas that went over to full-time bingo included the Chequers St Albans and the Essoldo Watford.

In the 1960s, mainstream films were released to either the ABC or Rank circuits, still for one week runs outside of London's West End and major provincial cities. Occasional longer runs of films like *The Bridge on the River Kwai* and *Dunkirk* had been seen in the 1950s

but from habit audiences tended to flock to films in the first week of showing. The fall in cinema attendances continued, annual admissions dropping from 501 million in 1960 to 193 million in 1970. The number of cinemas halved from 3,034 to 1,529.

There was still sufficient confidence left for some cinemas to be modernised throughout, like the Studio at Borehamwood, or in part (mainly the foyers), as happened at the County Hertford. The Granada circuit took over the Regent Bishop's Stortford and gave it a new name and a fresh look but soon switched it over to full-time bingo. During the 1960s it became obvious that most cinemas were too large. It was uneconomic to heat and otherwise maintain such large spaces and it was depressing for audiences to be scattered in handfuls around a vast auditorium.

Subdivision into two or more smaller cinemas seemed to be the answer. In the 1970s, major circuit cinemas were converted into three-screen 'film centres'. Non-inflammable safety film had become standard in the early 1950s and now new equipment had been introduced, requiring only one projector per screen that could basically run itself, with the programme on large reels on a 'tower' or horizontally placed on a 'platter' or 'cakestand'. The remarkable interior of the Embassy Waltham Cross was crassly obliterated in its conversion to three very plain new auditoria (fortunately, one can still visit another former Embassy, now the Odeon, at Esher, Surrey, to enjoy a very similar decorative scheme although it, too, is partly spoilt by recent subdivision.) A compromise at Berkhamsted split the Rex into bingo hall and two small cinemas.

Hit films like *Percy* and *Women in Love* were now being given standard two-week runs in many towns but in three-screen cinemas they could stay even longer, moved to a smaller screen. A smash hit like *Jaws* played at some cinemas for several months. At the same time, even the biggest cinemas resorted to showing 'sexploitation' films like *Flesh Gordon*

Closure of cinemas in Hertfordshire 1945-

1953 Sawbridgeworth Cinema	1968 Watford Essoldo
1954 Watford Plaza	1969 Stevenage Astonia
1957 Rickmansworth Odeon	1972 Hoddesdon Pavilion
1958 Bishop's Stortford Phoenix	Waltham Cross Regent
Buntingford Cosy	1973 Hatfield Curzon
1959 Cheshunt Central	1973 St Albans Gaumont
North Watford Odeon	1977 Bishop's Stortford Granada
Barnet Gaumont	Hitchin Regal
Harpenden State	Letchworth Palace
Hertford Castle	1979 Ware Astoria
1960 Tring Regal	1980 Watford Carlton
Berkhamsted Court	1981 Elstree Studio 70
Hemel Hempstead Luxor	1982 Hertford County
Radlett Cinema	1983 Harpenden Embassy
Stevenage Publix	Welwyn Garden City Embassy
1961 Standon Regal	Watford Odeon (three screens)
Welwyn Pavilion	1985 Baldock Astonia
Hemel Hempstead Princess	1988 Berkhamsted Rex (two screens) (scheduled
1963 Rickmansworth Picture House	to re-open late 2002)
Hitchin Hermitage	1993 Waltham Cross Cannon (three screens)
Watford Odeon	1994 Stevenage Cannon (two screens)
1965 St Albans Chequers	1995 St Albans Odeon (four screens)
1966 Barnet Regal	1996 Watford ABC (two screens)
1967 Barnet Essoldo	2000 Royston Priory
Potters Bar Ritz	

and *Come Play With Me*, often in an attempt to boost attendances in slack periods such as early December.

Cinema-goers became increasingly selective, partly because admission prices had risen so much. Only the main feature mattered, so double bills, shorts and supporting features vanished: a single film with advertising and trailers was shown, enabling two evening screenings with separate performances replacing the time-honoured continuous show. Regular children's Saturday shows declined in the face of television's programmes, then ceased. A ban on smoking was introduced, at first applied to one side of many auditoria, then throughout.

Apart from a sharp rise in 1978, fuelled by a raft of box-office successes led by *Star Wars*, attendances continued their decline, with the arrival of video threatening to wipe out picture-going altogether: a night in with a rented tape was a far cheaper and more flexible alternative. The Odeon Barnet even established a video outlet in the foyer. The future of films in cinemas had never looked bleaker. More cinemas closed, even some of those converted to three screens. Press and display advertising was cut back. Minute advertisements in local papers created a poor impression.

In 1978, the infrastructure of British film exhibition was scathingly criticised by Ascanio Branca, head of 20th Century-Fox in Britain: "No country in Europe is so badly served as Britain as to the condition of its theatres. Many of the multi-auditoria put up here are lousy. There are continual complaints about sound and comfort. It is pitiful... [British exhibitors] have no faith in the business."

New cinemas and additional screens in Hertfordshire 1945-

1960 Hemel Hempstead Odeon (1 screen, 1,148 seats) [closed]

1972 Waltham Cross Embassy (subdivided into three cinemas) [closed]

1973 St Albans Odeon (subdivided into three cinemas) [closed]

Stevenage ABC (2 screens, 522 seats) [closed]

1974 Barnet Odeon (now London Borough) (subdivided into three cinemas, then five from 1992)

Watford Odeon (subdivided into three cinemas) [closed]

1976 Berkhamsted Rex (subdivided into two small cinemas and bingo) [closed but re-opening late 2002 restored to single auditorium for cinema/events]

1980 Watford Empire (subdivided into two cinemas) [closed]

1991 Hatfield UCI (9 screens, 2,013 seats)

1995 Hemel Hempstead Odeon (8 screens, 1,651 seats)

1996 Watford Warner (8 screens, 2,026 seats)

Stevenage Cineworld (12 screens, 2,167 seats – four further screens being added in 2002)

Letchworth Broadway (subdivided into three screens)

1999 Borehamwood Cinema (4 screens, 590 seats)

2000 Bishop's Stortford Cineworld (6 screens, 1,237 seats)

The British public continued to abandon the big screen – admissions dropped from 101 million in 1980 to an all-time low of 54 million in 1984.

The two largest surviving cinema operators, Rank (Odeon) and EMI (owner of the old ABC and Shipman and King circuits) continued to cut back (although EMI did take over the small, poorly-located two-screen Empire Watford in 1976). The decline in attendances was exacerbated by the reduced number of cinemas that people could visit. Single-screen sites at Hertford and Welwyn Garden City were closed by EMI. Rank even sold the three-screen Odeon in the centre of Watford, leaving the county's largest town ridiculously under-served by only the Empire.

The loss of some cinemas caused a considerable uproar. The proposed demolition of the Palace Letchworth after its closure in 1977 was much criticised by those who thought it was of historic importance (forgetting that it had been rebuilt in 1924) when in fact it was the Broadway, still being taken for granted, that was the cinematic jewel in their midst.

Some people were mindful of what was being lost. In 1967, the cinema organ made an unexpected comeback in Hertfordshire – at the Plough Inn at Great Munden. A professional organ builder, Gerald Carrington, took over the

public house when his father died, and installed the Compton organ from the Gaumont Finchley, north London, in the lounge bar. The organ has become a popular attraction – normally played on Friday, Saturdays and Sundays with concerts by well-known organists on occasion.

In 1972, the Department of the Environment had listed two London cinemas and over the years many others have been listed for their architectural or social significance. But it was not until 1988 that the Rex Berkhamsted was spot-listed in the face of damaging proposed changes, with the Odeon Barnet following in 1989.

Return of the audience

In 1985, attendances recovered to total 72 million, partly due to a well-organised all-industry promotional exercise called British Film Year and partly due to a group of films – *Ghostbusters, Gremlins, Beverly Hills Cop* – that appealed to audiences. This recovery was then boosted by the arrival of the multiplex.

British exhibitors and leisure operators were well aware that the multiplex cinema had revitalised film exhibition in North America but there was doubt over whether the idea would work in this country, particularly because of the high cost of land. However, Bass Leisure, in developing the Point leisure complex at Milton Keynes, wanted a multiplex and linked up with a leading US chain, American Multi-Cinema, to obtain one. AMC decided to import its operating practices wholesale to this country rather than adapt to local conventions. It was rewarded when the 10-screen cinema at the Point, opened in October 1985, achieved one million admissions within the first year.

This led to a flurry of multiplexes, almost entirely opened by American companies, usually either in new (mostly out-of-town) shopping centres or alongside motorways so that they could draw audiences from a wide area (Milton Keynes, of course, is close to the M1). The minimum base for a British multiplex in 1990 was a catchment area of 200,000-300,000 people within a 20-minute drive. This contributed to the demise of the town centre cinemas, as did one-way systems and pedestrian precincts which appeared unsafe at night.

Most of the early British multiplexes were built in the Midlands and North where land was cheaper and more sites were available, but the South followed as the profitability of operating these cinemas became evident. Hertfordshire was ripe for such development with the M1, A1(M) and M25 motorways crossing the county, even though it lacked major city centres other than Watford. The Galleria retail development at Hatfield over the A1(M) attracted the UCI chain (a partnership of the Universal and Paramount film companies). Further north on the A1(M), Cine-UK (a British company) opened a multiplex at Stevenage. The Woodside leisure development at Garston, north of Watford, was well positioned to serve both the town and visitors from the M1 and M25 – it attracted a Warner multiplex. A new leisure park at Hemel Hempstead near the busy A41 included an Odeon multiplex while a smaller scheme at Bishops Stortford (handy for the M11) brought public cinema back to that town after a gap of over twenty years with a rel-

atively modest six-screen venture by Cine-UK. The only failure was an independent four-screen cinema in the centre of Borehamwood and this has been relaunched by a more powerful operator.

Most multiplexes have succeeded, particularly by catching the imagination of the young. They have emphasised soft drinks and freshly popped popcorn as part of the cinema-going experience, with holes in the armrests for containers. Vast screens, loud surround sound, well-drilled staff, computerised box-offices with advance booking and high standards of cleanliness have contributed to their appeal. Most sites offer secure (often open air) parking, and are linked to chain restaurants, fast food establishments and low-brow leisure facilities. Multiplexes offered massive choice: cinemagoers could decide what to see when they arrived, confident that most, if not all, of the current releases would be on offer. Saturday morning childrens' shows even reappeared. However, the spread of the American-style movie-going experience of the multiplex has been accompanied by an increased enthusiasm for watching Hollywood films.

Many old-fashioned cinemas, including some in nearby town centres, closed because of new multiplexes. The Odeon St Albans, which still made a profit, was shut in an attempt to force cinemagoers to support the new Odeon multiplex at Hemel Hempstead some miles away. The two-screen cinema in central Watford competed with the outlying new Warner for a few months before switching off the projectors for good. At Letchworth, the amenity value of having a local cinema was recognised and the Broadway, still a large, single-screen cinema, was lavishly converted to three screens (while retaining much of its historical character) by an unusual partnership between cinema owner and local authority, enabling it to survive despite the arrival of the multiplex at nearby Stevenage.

Some privately-run independent cinemas hung on, usually due to the dedication of their proprietors. The Priory at Royston was remote enough from multiplex competition to keep going as a single screen but the retirement of its operators brought to the fore the potential of the site for redevelopment, which was far greater than the rent that could be obtained from a new lessee. A campaign to save the cinema was launched but failed.

Admission totals to UK cinemas have climbed steadily (except for a slight blip in 1995) from that nadir of 54 million in 1985 to 156 million in 2001, the highest figure for twenty-nine years. Although certain areas of the country are widely recognised to have too many multiplex cinemas, those in Hertfordshire have proven to be well spaced out and profitable. There may not be much scope for further multiplexes in the county but a four or five screen city-centre development in Watford could be profitable and St Albans teeters on the edge of gaining a multiplex which ought to be commercially viable.

The seventeen years since the first edition of this book have seen momentous changes to the cinema scene in Hertfordshire amounting to its complete revitalisation. Older people tend to mourn the passing of the traditional High Street cinema but few that survived were well suited to meet the changes in the film market. At least the restoration of the auditorium of the listed Rex Berkhamsted for cinema and other uses promises to provide a splendid living memorial to the era of the picture palace.

The next fifteen or twenty years are unlikely to offer as much change as the period since 1985 but they will undoubtedly have their share of new and unpredictable developments.

Note

This volume salutes all the cinemas, past and present, of Hertfordshire, including those in Barnet (now a Greater London Borough though postally still in the county) and Potters Bar (formerly Middlesex). It deals with dedicated cinema operations but mentions some public halls and civic centres where films were an occasional feature in the early days or are part of a wider range of activities today. It should be noted, though, that films were also shown at Ashwell's Village Hall, Bushey's Village Hall, Codicote's Peace Memorial Hall, Furneux Pelham's Village Hall, Hexton's Village Hall, at Knebworth, and at Redbourn's Public Hall. Redbourn Village Hall (same as Public Hall?) seems to have turned into a cinema during the 1930s under a Mr Harding. It showed films once a week from 1946 to 1958 when it was managed by John Heather (who included very short films he had himself shot of children waving as they arrived for a film show and of the Harpenden Carnival).

There are several references to pre-decimal prices when twelve pence (12d) made one shilling (1/-) and twenty shillings made £1. 1/6d is one shilling and sixpence (the equivalent of 7½p now), etc.

BALDOCK

Monday 22 September 1913
Baldock Cinema
34 White Horse Street

T he first purpose-built cinema in Baldock opened with a three-day programme that included a film version of Sir Walter Scott's *Ivanhoe*. The silent films were accompanied by piano and violin and the shows featured live performers – comedians, singers, wooden shoe dancers, etc. "Local topicals" were sometimes shown – in the first week there was footage of the Baldock and Hitchin Bank Holiday Fêtes and the *North Herts Mail* reported: "Roars of laughter rang through the building as people in the audience recognised their acquaintants, the pictures containing some splendid animated photos of residents in both towns."

There were approximately 400 seats on a single sloping floor. The screen was situated at the front of the building by the main entrance, which was set back from the road. The early policy was an evening show at 8pm with extra shows at 3pm and 6pm on Saturdays and changes of programme each Monday and Thursday.

In the late 1920s Noel A. Ayres became proprietor and manager of the Baldock Cinema through the Baldock Cinema Company. A café was built alongside, to the right, around 1929. It also sold sweets and provided a business occupation for Mrs Ayres while the flat above became the living quarters of the Ayres family. In 1937 the Cinema claimed 500 seats and prices ranged from 5d to 1/3d.

Business was so encouraging that Mr Ayres opened a new, larger cinema in the town, the Astonia, and for a year or so both cinemas operated until it became clear the older building was no longer viable. It had closed by 1939 and was used for storage during the war. It was still standing in 1985, next to the Post Office, as the premises of DDB Electrical Ltd. while the former café had become a hairdressing salon. By 1991 the building was boarded up, and it has since been demolished and replaced by a new edifice.

The words "Baldock Cinema" could still be made out in 1985 on the top of the building it had formerly occupied. (Photograph by Allen Eyles.)

1938
Astonia
High Street

T his was the second Astonia opened by Noel Ayres, the first being at Stevenage, and in both cases the architect was H. V. J. Dutton. (This cinema's precise opening date remains elusive as it seems to have advertised only in the local *Garden City Advertiser*; it was certainly appearing there by the start of January 1939 but the 1938 editions cannot be consulted at the British Library due to conservation work, the 1937 editions have been mislaid, and the newspaper does not seem to have been preserved anywhere in Hertfordshire.)

Built on the edge of the town centre, facing a bend in the road, the Astonia made a striking impression with its streamlined frontage – a deep central recess with curved glazed wings and canopy projecting the full width. The 810-seat auditorium lay across the site with the screen at right angles to the road. There was no balcony. Twin 'love seats' were placed in the back row. The ceiling is recalled as having been louvered with concealed lighting that threw shafts of light downwards (a device that was much later seen at the Curzon Phoenix in London's West End).

The Baldock Astonia was not in a strong position for booking films and it had to play them three weeks or more after they had been seen in Letchworth or Hitchin. Consequently, films rarely ran more than three days and by 1966 generally changed every two days. Then, from Wednesday 11 October 1967, bingo replaced films on Wednesdays and Fridays. Bingo next came in on Sunday afternoons from 7 January 1968, spreading to Thursdays from 20 (or 27) June 1968, and Saturdays from 18 January 1969. Films had definitely taken a back seat, playing only on Sundays and the traditionally poor Monday and Tuesday evenings, so that it was no surprise when bingo took over all the time after a three-day run of a children's holiday attraction, *Jack the Giant Killer* (supported by *Ride the Wind*), which ended on Tuesday 30 December 1969.

Unfortunately, bingo did not prove a lasting salvation for the building as the Astonia closed on Sunday 30 June 1985, having run up losses of £400 per week. It was sold by Martin Ayres, son of its original proprietor, who sadly commented, "My father built it and I am destroying it, but there was nothing else I could do. We were losing money rapidly and paying about £40,000 in tax." It had been demolished by spring 1986 and the new owners of the site, Richard Daniels Developments of Langdon, replaced it with a block of flats for senior citizens called Astonia Court.

The Astonia Baldock in 1985. (Photograph by Allen Eyles.)

The auditorium of the Astonia Baldock in 1938. (Courtesy of Martin Ayres.)

BARNET

Thursday 26 December 1912

Cinema Palace / Barnet Cinema / Gaumont

122 High Street, High Barnet

O pened on Boxing Day (the same date as the Rink at Finchley) in the commercial heart of Barnet, the Cinema Palace had a single sloping floor with a white arched ceiling and was sufficiently well appointed to attract 'carriage folk'. It became more simply known as the Barnet Cinema from 9 October 1926 and later in the month a balcony was opened and the orchestra for accompanying silent films was greatly augmented. Talkies arrived with Norma Shearer and Lewis Stone in *The Trial of Mary Dugan* for a three-day run from Monday 17 February 1930 supported by the Empire News (silent), The Ideal Cine-Magazine (silent), and Norton-Baker and his Melody Princesses (on the stage: count them, "17 – Instrumentalists – 17"). At the same time the Cinema had been redecorated in an 'atmospheric' manner with representations of prominent Egyptian palaces, mosques and tombs. Patrons were invited to see the new apparatus for talking films in the operating booth during the mornings. Variety and the orchestra continued to be part of each show instead of a second feature until double bills quickly became the fashion.

The Cinema closed for a week's redecoration in early July 1933 and seems to have lost its Egyptian touches then. At some later point, probably in 1934, the original tall frontage with a curved entrance arch and rounded top (not illustrated) was reconstructed in a plainer contemporary style, with a café and dance hall over the entrance, while the auditorium seems to have undergone similar modernisation.

The Odeon circuit acquired the Cinema around December 1936 and recorded its seating as 919 in the stalls plus 119 in the circle – totalling 1,038. It was, of course, secondary to the new, larger Odeon down the road, although in a more central site. It became an outlet for the weekly Gaumont release and, after the Gaumont circuit was amalgamated with Odeon, this paved the way for the eventual re-naming of the theatre as the Gaumont from 10 January 1955. However, its exterior acquired the name of Coronet for one evening when it was relocated to the fictitious town of Barlow for an exterior scene in the Rank Organisation's thriller *Eye Witness* (1956) in which Donald Sinden's safe robber kills a cinema manager and is seen outside by Muriel Pavlow as he makes his escape.

Four years later the Gaumont was

The Gaumont (ex-Cinema) Barnet in the summer of 1959.

The auditorium of the Barnet Cinema (later Gaumont), circa December 1936.

deemed surplus to requirements and (like the North Watford Odeon) put up for auction on 22 April 1959 while it was still in operation. Closure followed on 8 August 1959 after a week's run of *The Mouse that Roared* plus *Juke Box Rhythm*. It was demolished in 1961 and a Waitrose supermarket put up in its place. This has now become an Iceland store.

Monday 27 April 1925

Hippodrome / New Barnet Kinema / New Barnet Picture Theatre / Regal

Lytton Road, New Barnet

The existing Assembly Rooms which stood on this site (and, see Introduction, apparently hosted a historic demonstration of moving pictures) were converted into a small cinema called the Hippodrome for M. P. Lawrence. The first programme had

Bryant Washburn in *Marriage à la Carte* plus Hoot Gibson in *Blinky*, with prices from 6d to 1/6d. Even with valuable prizes for having the lucky programme numbers (you could win a silver brush, a comb and mirror set), the venture seems to have ground to a halt on Saturday 18 July 1925.

Three months later, on Saturday 10 October 1925, a new proprietor, F. H. Melhuish, re-launched the building as the New Barnet Kinema after redecoration and re-equipping – a well-known soprano, Ethel Kernish, was engaged to accompany the first show of Bebe Daniels in *Miss Bluebeard* plus Chaplin's *The Floorwalker*. Mr Melhuish was sufficiently encouraged by the response to close down the Kinema on Saturday 29 May 1926 for re-building as a proper picture house.

Re-opening was on Thursday 11 November that year and seating had been greatly increased to 600 on the ground floor and 150 in the gallery. The decor included a ceiling painted to represent the firmament, showing stars, a rising moon, and day dawning in the east. It was now called the New Barnet Picture Theatre. Although slightly out of the way down a side street, it was very close to New Barnet railway station and provided a useful amenity for the immediate area, being more than a mile away from the cinema in High Barnet.

Then in September 1933 there was a change of name to Regal. It closed again on Saturday 26 June 1937 for further enlargement and modernisation to plans by the architectural practice of Howes and Jackman for proprietors A. W. and R. B. Green. The frontage was reconstructed to give a simple modern look rather in the style popularised by many Odeons. It was clad in warm biscuit-coloured tiles with rounded corners, a split-level, slightly protruding green upper edge, wide green bands in a black base, and an orange vertical bar over each of the two small windows. A modern name sign was mounted in the centre with a flagpole above. The Regal re-opened on Monday 11 October 1937 with a three-day run of *Wings of the Morning* (Henry Fonda in early Technicolor) plus *Career Woman* with Claire Trevor.

James C. Robertson, now living in Tunbridge Wells, attended Barnet's cinemas as a boy during the Second World War. "I have no particular memories of this cinema, except that it was seen by us as nothing special in prestige terms. I usually went there only if I had not seen the film at any of the other cinemas. The only films I recall seeing there were *The Adventures of Martin Eden* and *Squadron Leader X*, neither of which have I seen since, which suggests to me that it was indeed at the bottom end of the market. New Barnet itself struck me as rather drab and austere compared to the rest of the town, and the cinema was not somewhere I looked forward to visiting."

It was an independent cinema playing second run to the circuit theatres around or showing films that they did not want, and it had a struggle to survive as cinema attendances generally plummeted. The strain showed. One former patron, Patricia Nicholls, observes: "When you arrived at the cinema, the manager went into the box to issue a ticket, later catching you at the auditorium door to tear it in half before showing you to your seat. If there was a group of people, you were processed in batches. Later he served ices and drinks in the interval. It was a real one-man show."

By the early 1950s, Patricia Nicholls recalls that, of all the Barnet cinemas, the Regal was the most dangerous to attend. "I was more threatened in that cinema, with perverts finding subtle ways to touch your body. On one such occasion I went through

The Regal Barnet as the Vogue Bingo and Social Club in 1970.

hell trying to tell my friend to come out to the toilet with me so that I could tell her and we could go to another part of the auditorium. But she kept insisting she didn't need to go."

In the late 1950s and early 1960s the Regal adopted an adventurous policy of showing some art house programmes as well as gaining better fare by agreeing to extended runs with separate performances at increased prices (*Gigi* managed six weeks, *Around the World in 80 Days* stayed two).

But this could not make up for the weeks when the cinema had nothing that audiences wanted to see or had not already seen. The Regal closed on 28 July 1966 with *The Wonderful World of the Brothers Grimm*, having been acquired by the Classic group who turned it over immediately to Vogue Bingo. It later became a Mecca bingo hall until closure in 1988. Sold to a developer the following year, the building suffered several years of disuse. After failed attempts to turn it into a health club and nightclub, it became a snooker hall, then a Qasar laser war games centre from 1994 until circa 1997. The building was demolished a couple of years later and the site is now occupied by the nine flats of Clivedon Court, erected in 1999 by Michael Shanly Homes, with open space for car parking at the rear. However, a reminder of the past is provided by one of the businesses in the parade of shops opposite, called Regal Shoes.

Wednesday 15 May 1935

Odeon

Western Parade, Underhill, Great North Road

In its early days of expansion, Odeon Theatres had been intent on building a new cinema at the junction of Cat Hill and Brookhill Road in East Barnet but the plans drawn up by architects Yates, Cook and Darbyshire in the summer of 1933 came to nothing (the downward sloping site is now occupied by the flats of Brookhill Court). Later, at a site on the Great North Road, about a mile away, work began on a new County cinema for the same directorate that had created the Hermitage in Hitchin and County at Hertford, including architect Edgar Simmons and builder John Ray. This was a good half mile from the centre of High Barnet although close to the terminus of the Northern Line branch of London Underground. It was located at an important road junction, the site allowed extensive provision for car parking while a forecourt enabled drivers to stop and drop off passengers outside the entrance.

In March 1935 the name 'County' was covered over on the notice board at the front of the half-completed building and the name 'Odeon Theatre' was painted in huge letters on the side of the pitched roof facing the top of the hill. The Odeon circuit had taken over.

The Odeon Barnet had a contract figure of £29,130 and there were 1,010 seats in the stalls and 543 in the balcony, providing a total of 1,553. Unusually, the cinema originally drew power from its own diesel engines, relying on the mains for secondary supply. Its exterior closely copied that of the County at Hertford, opened nearly two years earlier. The front elevation looks lower at Barnet but there are the same line of Moorish arches, red brick wings with X-shaped diaper patterns and raised vertical lighting fixtures with the same art deco pattern on the glazing. The low side extensions, containing exits and queueing corridors, were repeated at Barnet with steps marked by lanterns on pylons. Main name signs in the trademarked Odeon style were mounted horizontally on each wing at Barnet and supplemented by smaller vertical signs at the edge of the side walls.

Inside, the Odeon had elegant ticket windows facing each other at each side. Matching staircases led up to the balcony foyer where it was possible to look down to the ground floor via a light well which had a suspended light fitting. The auditorium at Barnet had a great deal in common with that at Hertford including the same style of laylight in the ceiling and acoustic wallboards in place of plaster on the side walls and ceiling. However, the Odeon had a lower ceiling and richer, jazzier detailing than the County without its ponderous suspended light fittings along the side walls. The laylight was in a stretched octagonal pattern which the architect used as a motif, seen also in the ground floor windows on the brick towers and, at Barnet, in the shape of the light well between balcony foyer and main foyer. (The Hermitage at Hitchin had a somewhat different exterior but displayed the Moorish arches and diaper work decoration of the brickwork, while its interior more resembled the County than the Odeon.)

The Barnet auditorium was a rich blend of art deco and Moorish motifs. Odeon took over in sufficient time to have the circuit pattern of carpet laid down and to put Odeon clocks on both side walls, as well as to cancel plans for an organ (the instrument was little favoured by the circuit). The original seating was in alternate red and blue upholstery, which was not standard Odeon practice.

The Odeon was certainly the leading cinema in the Barnet area. James C. Robertson recalls: "My chief memory is that, unlike the other cinemas, the Odeon had a uniformed usher in the foyer. As with all the other cinemas in the area, if I was on my own and either film carried an 'A' certificate [which required anyone under 16 to be accompanied by an adult], I asked an adult, almost always a man, to take me in with him at the cashier's desk – 'Will you take me in, mister?' Only very occasionally was I unable to gain admission by this means. Once inside, the adult and I always separated. The cinema staff must have known what was going on, but never once at any of the cinemas was the adult challenged, even though what he was doing was technically illegal. The usher at the Odeon was pretty keen-eyed but, even so, I remember only one occasion when I was unable to get in with adult help. This was a film called *Social Enemy No. 1* – about venereal disease, a phrase I heard but had not a clue what it meant. In general, I was vaguely aware that the Odeon was posh and that I was expected to be on my best behaviour. I think the ticket prices were slightly dearer than at the other Barnet cinemas, for which reason my mother was not too keen on my going there. Films I particularly remember seeing there were *Holiday Inn* with Bing Crosby and Fred

The Odeon Barnet in 1935.

Astaire, *Star Spangled Rhythm, Thank Your Lucky Stars* and *Going My Way*."

The Odeon outlasted all its competitors and in 1974 was converted to three screens at a cost of £50,000. This involved creating two 130-seat cinemas underneath the balcony. These opened on 10 March 1974 with *A Touch of Class* and *Fantasia*. The circle, still with 543 seats, became the main cinema using the old screen. Unfortunately, the conversion work downstairs extended obtrusively beyond the circle front to accommodate a projection suite that throws the picture onto the screens of the mini-cinemas from behind via mirrors. Projection from the rear in the conventional manner would have taken up too much space and reduced the number of seats to an uneconomic level. Sitting in the balcony, it was possible to see only the upper two thirds of the original proscenium arch and the screen was raised accordingly.

Following the conversion, the laylights over the circle continued to light up during intervals but the main, octagonal one in the centre of the ceiling remained dark to avoid illuminating the unsightly disused area in front of the balcony. The uplights in the niches of the splay walls were replaced by plain ventilation grilles and new lights pointing forward to illuminate the curtains.

Externally, the Odeon long ago had lost the lamps on top of the posts by the side exit steps. By 1984, and probably from the time of tripling, the two attractive vertical light fittings mounted on the side towers had been removed and the recesses behind filled in with new brickwork. When the conversion took place, a new wide 'lightbox' or readograph was mounted above the canopy, backlighting the lettering giving the current choice of programmes. The canopy front

had carried changeable lettering but was filled in with the worlds 'ODEON FILM CENTRE' permanently added across the front.

The original set of four neon name signs lasted until the spring of 1985 when a single name sign in cheap red plastic letters appeared at top left in the lightbox. Inside a new counter, set across the back of the main foyer, sold tickets and refreshments while, to the right, the Odeon embraced the video age with a cassette shop that used as its cash desk one of the two original wood-panelled box-offices with windows that faced each other across the hall. The pendant light fitting in the opening to the balcony foyer had by this time been replaced with a cheap-looking series of tubular light shades.

In 1988 the Odeon reverted externally

The auditorium of the Odeon Barnet in 1935.

to single-screen status momentarily for the benefit of the company making the film *Buster,* set in 1963, so that it could be photographed displaying *Lawrence of Arabia* as its current sole attraction.

The Odeon's future became uncertain when its owners, the Rank Organisation, closed another of its cinemas four miles away, the Gaumont Finchley, and planned to open a new cinema with two or more screens on the site. This never happened and Rank decided to invest in Barnet instead by creating extra screens.

On 13 October 1989, after plans were submitted to further subdivide the main auditorium and to remove or hide all the original decoration, the Odeon was given listed building status by the Department of the Environment on the recommendation of English Heritage. Rank was refused permission to alter the auditorium because it "would involve unacceptable damage to the original and unique interior features" but the company, in appealing against this decision, claimed that the Odeon's long-term viability was at stake and that its proposed alterations would not damage or destroy the decorative features, some of which would be protected by see-through panels (although it seems that the original proscenium and splay walls would have been hidden behind a new screen set up close to the balcony front). A public inquiry was held and the Inspector in his report sided with Rank.

Nevertheless, the alterations that followed did both preserve and keep on display most of the decorative features of the auditorium. The entire lower area in front of the balcony was roofed over so that a further cinema, which became operative on 18 December 1992 with 193 seats, could be established in the former front stalls, across the orchestra pit and in the lower part of the stage. This displayed no historic features.

The projector was installed at the back by enlarging the suite that contained the projectors serving the two small rear cinemas.

The area above the new downstairs cinema that lay behind the proscenium opening was used for a fifth screen which opened on 28 December 1992 with its own projection box. Long, narrow and very plain, this extended across the stage from one wing to the other and seated 162. It was reached by an upward flight of stairs at the end of a corridor down the right side of the building which also provided the access to the fourth cinema.

The original proscenium arch was blocked in to create a soundproof left-hand side wall of the fifth cinema and this meant that the screen, the speakers behind, and the curtains that faced the audience seated in the former balcony all had to come forward. These were contained within a new proscenium arch, shallower in depth, which replicated the main decorative elements of the old arch and stood just in front of where it had been. This was lit by a line of spotlights mounted across the flat roof of the new screen below. The roof descended on each side to expose in full the surviving decorative features on each splay wall, but the lower parts can be seen only from the sides of the former balcony. The seating now totalled 528.

In the foyer, a new paybox was set up. One of the two original pay boxes with frosted glass was used for collecting credit card bookings.

As part of a re-branding and modernisation exercise that spread across the Odeon circuit in the late 1990s, the company put up new-style silver Odeon name signs with blue backing that lit up at night: a large one was mounted on the canopy in place of the readograph; a smaller one was placed above the arches and two large ones appeared on the side and back of the flytower. Strips of blue neon were added to the brick wings of the frontage outlining where the vertical lighting features had once been seen. The current films were advertised using adhesive silver lettering which was mounted on a taller canopy, painted blue.

Proposed alterations to the foyer were refused listed building consent. Eventually a compromise was hammered out. Odeon paid for barriers to be created in the style of the bannisters and balustrading of the upper foyer to enclose the disabled ramps set up on each side of the forecourt (these then had to have an awkward extension on top to increase their height). A new outdoor paybox was established in the centre of the entrance, selling tickets to patrons before they entered the building. The levels of the ground floor foyer were drastically altered, with curving steps and disabled ramps on each side sweeping past the two renovated but now disused pay boxes fitted with frosted glass. Some inner doors were removed but some original columns in faux marble remained on view amid the raised wooden floor of the pic'n'mix confectionery area. A stylish wiry curving light fitting is now suspended in the opening to the balcony foyer. Upstairs, a new lighter-coloured decorative scheme has been introduced. The side and back walls of the balcony have been covered in drapes to improve the acoustics and make a more attractive impression, although the original art deco light fittings are retained and not obscured. The ceiling has been sealed and painted to create a more even impression and disguise the panels that had become warped with age. The colour scheme is not as subtle as that of 1935.

After the completion of refurbishment, the Odeon was officially re-opened by Emma Bunton, 'Baby Spice' of the all-girl pop group The Spice Girls, on 19 November 2000 with a plaque to note the occasion being placed on the wall of the balcony foyer. This appears alongside a plaque placed during the Centenary of Cinema celebrations in 1996 to recall the pioneering work of Birt Acres and Robert Paul in Barnet (mentioned in the Introduction).

In 2002, the Odeon Barnet remains one of the few 1930s Odeon cinemas to remain operative, although heavily subdivided. Its current seating figures are 528, 140, 150, 193 and 158.

Monday 31 October 1938

Dominion / Essoldo

235 East Barnet Road

Half a mile away from New Barnet and a mile away from the Odeon, the village of East Barnet had developed sufficiently to warrant a cinema of its own. As mentioned earlier, the Odeon circuit had found a site here before taking over the scheme that architect Edgar Simmons and builder John Ray had started building on the Great North Road. Now Simmons and Ray teamed up to develop a new cinema in East Barnet on a more central site than Odeon had contemplated. But, just as they had relinquished their County scheme to Odeon, so Simmons and Ray sold their latest scheme to the partnership of Albert Bacal and Nathan Lee which had created a small chain of Dominion cinemas at Southall, Harrow, Acton and elsewhere in the London area.

Simmons had died by the time construction started and F. E. Bromige, the notable architect who had designed the earlier Dominions for Bacal and Lee, provided site supervision while the cinema was built, essentially to its original design. The East

Barnet cinema took the Dominion name and seated a fairly modest 1,006. The exterior was very plain but the brickwork displayed the diaper treatment at each side as seen at Simmons' Barnet Odeon and County Hertford. Especially in the ceiling treatment, the auditorium showed marked similarities to the Odeon. It must have been difficult at times for picturegoers to remember which cinema they were sitting in.

The Dominion had a notable Monday evening start when Gracie Fields was the guest of honour who declared it open. A report in the Barnet press read: "The queue, four or five deep, of those hoping to gain admittance to the cinema stretched from the theatre to a considerable distance up Crescent Road. About fifteen minutes before the opening ceremony every seat in the cinema ... was taken. When Miss Fields appeared, crowds surged around her car, and with a struggle she and her party reached the sanctuary of the locked doors of the cinema foyer." The crowd became so massive that it blocked the road, and traffic had to be diverted down Brookhill Road.

On stage 'Our Gracie' sang 'The Biggest Aspidistra in the World' as well as a hit song of the time, 'Music, Maestro, Please'. She then invited the audience to have a "reet good do" and to sing the choruses with her. Once she had performed the opening ceremony, she retired to the café in the circle lounge. From there, she later stepped out onto the canopy, delighting the huge crowd outside when she sang 'Sally' to them.

James C. Robertson, who as a youngster during World War II lived in Potters Bar,

The Dominion East Barnet as the Essoldo in 1953.

recalls: "In terms of bus routes from Potters Bar, this cinema was rather off the beaten track, for which reason I went there less often than to the other [Barnet] cinemas. However, it had one advantage for me in that it was, I think, the only one in Barnet that opened on a Sunday, showing an old film, i.e. one that was a few years old. In this way I could sometimes see films I had heard of but had never had a chance of seeing. One such film made a strong impression upon me just on account of one scene. This was the 1939 *Of Mice and Men* and the scene was one in which the very old dog of an old man is taken out to be shot. The dog is seen being led docilely out of the bunkhouse and then the shot is heard. I was heartbroken at the time and even now when I see the same scene my heart always misses a beat and I remember the Dominion. The only other film I recall seeing there was the Arthur Askey vehicle, *King Arthur was a Gentleman*."

The cinema was large enough and modern enough to obtain the ABC circuit release on its first week of London suburban release in the absence of an ABC cinema in the Barnet area. It seems to have changed ownership a couple of times before passing to the large, Newcastle-based Essoldo circuit around 1947. By this time, according to Patricia Nicholls, "to the street pack it was often known as the 'Flea Pit'".

If their parents were not available, young children had to find adults to take them into programmes with 'A' certificates. Patricia Nicholls recalls visiting the Dominion. "I would have been about eleven/twelve years old. I remember hanging around outside with street pals waiting to get in [when the house was full] or be taken in, in cold, dark, foggy weather chilling you through, often to no avail. Maybe no one came out, releasing their seat, until it was too late – to pay after

the main film started was a waste of money. We would come again another day."

After the cinema was considerably re-vamped, this was reflected in a change of name to Essoldo on 22 January 1950.

In 1954, when the Rank Organisation balked at installing stereophonic sound in all its cinemas along with the new wide screen CinemaScope process that was being launched by 20th Century-Fox, the American film company responded by setting up a new circuit to show its films that included most of the Essoldo chain. The Essoldo East Barnet was in the very first batch of London suburban cinemas to show a film in CinemaScope – the Royal tour documentary, *Flight of the White Heron*, which opened on Monday 7 June 1954. Besides showing Fox CinemaScope films for the next few years, the Essoldo continued to screen many of the ABC circuit release programmes and so had plenty of popular films to show. After Fox patched up its quarrel with Rank in 1958 and the company's films returned to the Odeon and Gaumont in Barnet, the Essoldo combined the best of the ABC releases with off-circuit programmes and re-issue double bills. It bowed out on a high note with a two-week presentation of the hit musical *My Fair Lady* on its first general release after a long West End run. On the last night, Saturday 21 January 1967, the cinema was packed.

In a letter to the local press, H. Gowan wrote about that final evening: "The Essoldo was always a friendly place, and many old age pensioners went regularly – making a bee-line for the radiators in the cold weather. The Essoldo will be sadly missed. I saw many patrons stand up in their seats after most of the crowd had gone and gaze down at the blank screen, before walking slowly out. I and a few others watched the neon lights go out and went

The auditorium of the Dominion at East Barnet in 1938. Note the close similarities with the Odeon Barnet interior.

our way feeling a trifle sad – and remembering happy hours."

Frank Snart, who later ran cinemas himself, remembers it well: "During the 1950s, when I was a child, we went to the pictures virtually every Saturday afternoon. My father liked the Essoldo. His excuse was that he liked the sound there but I think it was its location. Most of the films my parents wanted to see were on the ABC release which in the main was picked up by the Essoldo and it was the easiest to get to from where we lived in Southgate, N14. So the Essoldo it was, and we always went to the show starting at around 4.30pm. The sound was superior to the other local halls.

"The entrance was up a number of steps and via the usual sets of double doors (green, I seem to remember) into the lobby, which was only about 8ft deep. The paybox

was located centrally on the wall dividing the lobby from the foyer. There were more sets of double doors into the foyer. Immediately behind the paybox but in the foyer was the sales kiosk. What was unusual was that, just beyond the kiosk, there was another set of four or five steps running right across the foyer, taking you up to another level, and, if I remember correctly, there was even a couple just before reaching the stalls doors. The reason for this was that the ground rose from the front of the building and the rear of the stalls was quite a bit higher than street level. The foyer had around the walls wooden panels up to waist height. Above that, the walls and ceilings were plastered with a stipple effect and were painted in bright pinks or cream. On the left-hand side of the foyer was a wide staircase leading up to the circle lounge and circle. On the half landing was quite an attractive large window frame with a rounded top.

"It was really difficult to see the auditorium at all, even with the house lights raised. There was some trough lighting in the main ceiling around the edge of the decorative effect which looked as if it was made out of fibre board together with all of the main ceiling. (I once went into the manager's office just off the circle lounge and the walls in there were made from the same board.)

"The features in the splay walls were lit from the bottom. Under the circle there were just two circular light fittings about 18 inches across, fitted flush to the ceiling. A further two were in the main ceiling behind the decorative effect and just in front of the projection box. In all, the auditorium was a bit seedy. There were no screen tabs. One just sat and looked at a blank screen in the intervals, though it was lit by either red or blue footlights. This made the place seem rather sad. (Tom Barker, the chief at the Odeon Southgate, later suggested to me that the tabs were probably removed at the time of the CinemaScope installation, there not being sufficient room behind the pros arch to clear the wide screen.) However, in true Essoldo fashion, projection and sound were excellent and I later learned it was equipped with four-track magnetic sound.

"The hall was of quite modest size. There were just three blocks of seats across: two side blocks, then gangways and one centre block. The circle was a little unusual in that the back row extended right across the whole width and against the back wall.

There was the usual entrance from the circle lounge into the central crossover, and the two fire exits were positioned at either end of this gangway. These exits led through double doors onto flat landings that extended beyond the auditorium walls and through another set of double doors down iron fire escape-type staircases out into the open air. One had the impression that the place really had been built on the cheap.

"It was very sad when it closed in 1967. Whilst it was in the early stages of being demolished, I went down to the site one Sunday afternoon, walked around to the stage end, and peered through a hole in the old horn chamber [the space behind the screen containing the speaker], which had been constructed from asbestos sheeting. The main roof was off and the ceiling was lying in bits in the stalls. I could see the projection ports in the back wall above what was left of the circle. For once the auditorium walls were exposed to daylight and they were black – no doubt, from years of being subjected to nicotine smoke. I suspect that the hall never received another coat of paint from the day it was opened. For a moment, I had some crazy notion of offering the demolition contractors ten shillings for the large red Essoldo neon sign that was mounted high on the front of the building. Quite what I would have done with it, I don't know! Even now, some thirty-five years on, I still have very fond memories of the place and still feel a certain sadness at its passing."

Whereas every shopping centre needed a cinema to thrive in the 1930s, it had greater need of a supermarket by the 1960s and the Essoldo was demolished to make way for a branch of Budgens that continues to operate in 2002.

BERKHAMSTED

Spring 1911

Gem

Cowper Road

The Gem was merely a corrugated iron hut adapted for the display of moving pictures. Prior to this, films had been shown at the Town Hall and by Taylor's Royal Electric Coliseum de Luxe, a travelling show that had occupied Crooked Billet Meadow for a season from 9 June 1910 with an "interior ... fitted up in the most elaborate style that money and artistic study can produce" that even included a gallery.

The Gem was located on the right hand side of Cowper Road going up from the High Road, between the Sayers almshouses on the corner and the Wesleyan Methodist Church. There was nothing elaborate about its style. Plans show a capacity of 168 in twelve rows of fourteen places. A single projector, using the crude oxyhydrogen lighting method, beamed the picture down a "metal funnel" onto the rear of a l0 foot-wide rather transparent screen from a fireproof operating chamber located 15 feet away from the auditorium. Although it was safe, breakdowns were frequent and there was only a single pianist to hold the audience's attention.

As 'Beorcham' (the late Percy Birtchnell) recalled in the *Berkhamsted Review*, August 1967: "The Gem Picture Palace was a grand name for a corrugated iron building with a noisy gas engine and an unreliable projector. Kitty Wilkins, the pianist, competed with those early cinema pests, the sub-title announcers who droned away in the belief that no one else could read. The manager

was accustomed to returning the full price of admission when the projector jammed halfway through the performance. The audience faced the projector, seeing films on the back of a rather small and almost transparent screen. This method of projection led to some loss of clarity and later the films were shown on the matchboarded wall." And in the same journal's March 1984 issue, 'Beorcham' recalled, "Kitty Wilkins was paid 7/6d. [37½p] to play a piano which helped to drown the noise of the projector, which often broke down. 'Want a spanner, mate?' was a popular cry, and if there was a long wait the audience walked out and had their money back."

Mr Taylor was not deterred from returning with his travelling show on 8 June 1911. As 'Beorcham' has indicated, the position of the screen was changed. The Gem improved its presentation by reversing the seats, putting the back rows on a raised platform, and using the existing projection arrangement to throw the image further onto a much larger screen painted on the wall at the other end of the auditorium. This alteration is the likely explanation for a period of closure that lasted until Saturday 26 October 1912.

The Gem did not survive much longer. It was unable to compete with the new Picture Playhouse, quite apart from the efforts of its own manager, Albert Lake, to launch a rival cinema enterprise and recruit the Gem's staff (the same Mr Lake was charged with embezzling £50 owed to a Wardour Street film distributor).

The building saw some use as an auction showroom, then in March 1916 it was purchased for £300 by the gas company for use as a warehouse. Before they could move in, the Inns of Court took over and used the space for training and storage. However, it later passed to the gas company and became a storage space for appliances. The

Gem's outside paybox remained, unused for decades, until the 1950s. The whole corrugated iron structure was demolished in the early 1960s and its site was vacant in 1985. Two houses – Eastview and Westview – plus access space to the rear of High Street shops now occupy the general area.

Circa November 1912

Picture Playhouse
Prince Edward Street

A syndicate of local businessmen engaged an architect, Herbert A. Bowes of St Quintin Park, London, and had the stables of the King's Arms Hotel converted into a cinema seating 340 on a raked floor with a screen 12ft by 9ft. The projection box was above the entrance, supported by four columns at the head of some stone steps with the space underneath forming an open lobby. This cinema had not only a pianist but also a violinist plus occasional live acts. 'Beorcham' in the *Berkhamsted St*

The Court Berkhamsted.

Peter Parochial Review (September 1960) recalled: "We thought it a very sumptuous place, and the pianist and violinist had to work hard to compete with our applause as pictures of Tommies in the trenches came on the screen."

After a wobbly start, the Picture Playhouse soon prospered with new capital and new management and became inadequate to meet the demand. The larger Court was built close by as a replacement, just across the High Street from the start of Prince Edward Street. The Picture Playhouse closed on Saturday 17 March 1917, after which the seats were taken out to be used in the new cinema. Later enlarged and given a new front, the building became the King's Hall and was still functioning as such in the mid-1980s but has since been replaced by an office block, called Fells House in 2002.

Saturday 24 March 1917

Court
High Street (corner of Water Lane)

As at Hoddesdon and St Albans, a former brewery provided a site for a new cinema. Here the owner of the old disused brewery, David Pike, joined forces with the proprietors of the Picture Playhouse to open the Court Theatre for which plans were drawn up by London architect Ewen S. Barr (earlier responsible for the Hitchin Playhouse).

The Court took its name from the Inns of Court Officer Training Corps which was stationed at Berkhamsted during World War I. The war had greatly hindered completion of the cinema: the date 1916 had been optimistically emblazoned on the frontage and the stage was still not quite finished by the first night. Panels with paintings by an

The Court Berkhamsted after 1934 reconstruction.

The main foyer of the Court Berkhamsted after 1934 reconstruction.

Italian artist adorned the walls and there was seating for over 700 including the balcony and some family boxes.

The regimental band played on the opening night and the choice of name helped ensure the patronage of soldiers: indeed, the only reason it was able to open during World War I was the pressing need for entertainment for the servicemen stationed in the area. An early hand-coloured film, *The Growth of Plants*, was among those shown on the first night when live performers also entertained briefly. The first manager was C.W. Fox, transferred from the now defunct Picture Playhouse. The screen here measured 18ft by 13ft. Another effect of the war was the absence of men to form an orchestra and so an all-female group was formed to accompany the silent pictures.

'Beorcham' in 1960 recalled: "As a small boy I had a front seat at the opening performance, and was too thrilled by the magnificent surroundings to worry about the newly whitewashed screen, which was still damp and grey. Those were the days! We paid 2½d to attend the Saturday matinée, and the price sometimes included an orange or a bag of sweets. It was the age of slapstick comedy and thrilling serials. To see how the hero escaped from crocodiles or how the heroine was rescued when an express train was only half a yard away, we had to pay 2½d the following Saturday."

The front originally had an oriental dome that seemed out of place. Graham Greene in his autobiography *A Sort of Life* (1971) wrote: "The High Street was wide as many a market square, but its broad dignity

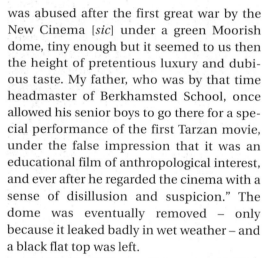

The auditorium of the Court Berkhamsted after 1934 reconstruction.

Thomas Grosch at the Christie organ of the Court Berkhamsted in 1935

was abused after the first great war by the New Cinema [*sic*] under a green Moorish dome, tiny enough but it seemed to us then the height of pretentious luxury and dubious taste. My father, who was by that time headmaster of Berkhamsted School, once allowed his senior boys to go there for a special performance of the first Tarzan movie, under the false impression that it was an educational film of anthropological interest, and ever after he regarded the cinema with a sense of disillusion and suspicion." The dome was eventually removed – only because it leaked badly in wet weather – and a black flat top was left.

By March 1930, the Shipman and King circuit had acquired the Court and in 1934 the company transformed it to plans by architect A. Belcham (of Howis and Belcham). Spreading onto adjacent land, its seating was raised from 624 to nearly 1,000 during five weeks of closure. Modern decorative grilles and concealed lighting were put in the auditorium and a Christie organ with an illuminated console on a lift was installed with the chamber for the organ pipes on the right-hand side (the organ was removed in 1937 to S & K's new Embassy

Waltham Cross). The Court also gained a new slim entrance block. It re-opened on 17 September 1934.

S & K then built the larger Rex and the Court became of secondary importance. It had retained its stage facilities and the Berkhamsted Amateur Operatic and Dramatic Society presented some shows there. Then the Berkhamsted Repertory Company was formed to take over the Court from Easter Monday 10 April 1939 for a season so successful that it remained a live theatre until the end of January 1940 when war-time conditions probably made it impossible to continue. Films returned in February. Then, as later, the Court usually changed programmes mid-week while the stronger attractions played the Rex and frequently lasted the whole week.

In 1955 the Court had to be temporarily closed because of electrical shortcomings. It also took to closing every June and July. After the John Wayne film *The Horse Soldiers* played a three-day run ending on Saturday 11 June 1960, the Court closed for its annual recess but a week before the scheduled re-opening the manager was told it would stay shut. It was sold and converted into a Tesco store which was badly damaged by fire in 1969. The site was cleared and the larger Tesco supermarket which replaced it is still there in 2002.

Monday 9 May 1938

Rex / Studio 1 / Rex

1 & 2 High Street
(corner of Three Close Lane)

The S & K circuit specialised in having pairs of cinemas in country towns, usually an older property and a larger one which it had specially built. Berkhamsted is an example. S & K took over the Court and later planned to build a second cinema at the eastern end of the High Street on the corner of Swing Gate Lane (the site, later used for a school, was first proposed for a cinema by Edward Greene, uncle of Graham and Sir Hugh Greene). S & K then acquired Egerton House, an old Tudor building, which was a better site at the same end of town but closer to the centre, with space for a large car park behind that had to be cut out of a steep incline. The circuit's leading cinemas were usually named Embassy but here Rex was decided upon. The cinema opened with the Shirley Temple vehicle, *Heidi*.

The architect was David E. Nye, who often worked for S & K. The cinema had a prominent entrance on the corner with an associated parade of five shops with flats above. Steps led up to five sets of double doors below a slightly curved canopy on which the name of the cinema was mounted. Above canopy level, there were tall windows set in a curve and neon mounted in vertical strips on the rendered columns to either side.

There was an exceptionally impressive and spacious double-height foyer with an art deco pendant chandelier suspended from a triple-coved ceiling. The floor had a striped pattern leading toward the auditorium. A rounded island paybox in wood and glass with chrome trim was set in the centre. Access to the stalls was provided by steps behind the paybox while the balcony was reached by stairs to each side. The side walls were painted in vertical bands to achieve a fluted effect: these emphasised the height, as did the tall blue-tinted art deco mirrors on the side of each staircase to the balcony.

Beyond the foyer, the layout at the Rex was rather unusual. The auditorium extended from the side road, Three Close Lane, across the site, behind the parade of shops. There proved to be insufficient room for a café in the circle lounge and so the rear stalls area was reduced to provide the necessary space. To keep down the ceiling height and provide the maximum seating in the balcony, the projection box was built high up outside the auditorium on rakers that extended through the back wall. Locals joked that the architect had forgotten to include a projection room in the first place. It had to be entered from an outdoor iron staircase that could become slippery and was only too visible from Three Close Lane. The inflammable nature of the nitrate film stock then being projected dictated that access to the projection room had to be outside the actual auditorium, but one would have expected an enclosed stairway.

As a result of the space taken up by the café, another unusual feature was that the circle had more seats than the stalls, which it barely overlapped. The overall total was 1,100. The design of the auditorium had a marine flavour with shell-like light fittings (illuminated from within) arranged on wavy bands on the side walls (Nye's Embassy at Fareham in Hampshire was very similar).

The Rex Berkhamsted in 1938.

There was also elaborate pierced grillework surrounding both the sides and top of the proscenium opening and a band of grillework covering a ventilation opening across the ceiling over the balcony as well as a lighting recess with scalloped edge over the front stalls. Who was responsible for the interior decoration is not known but it could well have been Mollo and Egan who worked with Nye on other S & K interiors.

The Rex first opened on Sundays from 15 January 1939 (the Court never did show films on Sundays). For thirty years or so, the cinema remained successful but it was too large by the 1970s. After a week's run of *The Amazing Mr Blunden* ending Saturday 6 January 1973, it was taken over by the Star Group which closed it for a week. Then from

Sunday 14 January, films were relegated to the first four days of the week when it was known as the Studio 1, while (from 18 January) bingo was played on the busy Thursday to Saturday period.

In 1976, Zetter's took over and spent more than £90,000 on alterations. The last film on the old screen was *Rollerball*, ending on Wednesday 7 April. The circle was divided to become the Rex 1 and 2 cinemas seating 263 and 163 respectively while the stalls went over to full-time bingo with the restaurant area being filled with fruit machines. The cinemas retained the main entrance where the side wall mirrors survived although the circular paybox and the central light fitting had gone. Bingo players entered the old café area and stalls via a new entrance on Three Close Lane. The shell fittings on the side walls were retained in both the cinemas (though not matched on the new inner walls) as well as in the bingo area. Rex 1 and 2 actually opened on Sunday 11 April with *Swinging Wives* plus *Sex in the Office* on 1 and *The Bruce Lee Story* plus *Somebody's Stolen our Russian Spy* on 2, but the official opening took place with the more respectable *Alice Doesn't Live Here Anymore* in Rex 1 before invited guests on Tuesday 13 April while Rex 2 was closed for the night (playing *Carry On Behind* from the next day). The subdivision of the building worked out satisfactorily from a business point of view as the cinemas continued showing films while in the hands of a succession of bingo operators.

However, the entire building closed on 28 February 1988 on expiry of the lease. The last films to be shown were *The Witches of Eastwick* and *Teen Wolf Two*. The owner had sold the site to a developer proposing to replace the cinema with offices and flats. The news of impending closure and threat of demolition stirred the Cinema Theatre

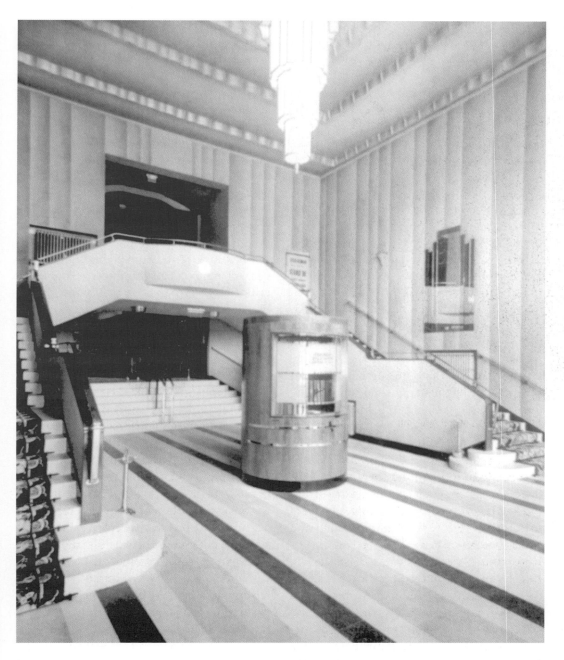

The superb foyer of the Rex Berkhamsted in 1938 with its island paybox, art deco pendant central light in stepped recess , directional floor pattern, tinted mirrors and fluted effect on the flat walls.

Association to make efforts to save the building and it was spotlisted Grade II by English Heritage two days before it shut down.

The new owners responded quickly by applying for permission to demolish the building and redevelop the site. This stimulated a local campaign to save the Rex as an arts centre and cinema, leaving the tricky question of how this would be financed. A public inquiry in 1989 was initially called off when the owners submitted new plans which might retain the cinema but in 1990 it was convened. A planning inspector for the Department of the Environment reported that the exterior formed part of the diverse nature of the street scene as an example of 1930s architecture while the interior features were of such quantity and quality as to merit the listing of the building. He declared that insufficient efforts had been made to continue the original use of the building. The Secretary of State for the Environment accepted his inspector's report, quashing the scheme to replace the building with offices.

Rival proposals surfaced in 1992: one by the owners to refurbish the façade and foyer and create offices around the cinema with the auditorium space serving as an atrium (preserving only the proscenium arch) and the other to restore the entire building and add a conference hall at the back.

Planning permission was granted in 1993 for the building to become offices with the twin cinemas in the balcony serving as lecture theatres and only the foyer and restaurant area being restored. Not surprisingly, this failed to receive listed building consent. The local council was forced to take steps to make the building more secure after a fire caused minor damage to the stage area in early 1994.

In 1997, a group called Friends of the Rex was formed to try to save the cinema while plans were lodged to turn it into a health club and the owners, Estates and General Property Company, attempted to have the building de-listed with the support of the local South West Herts Member of Parliament, Richard Page (who described the place as "an absolute disgrace and a dump" and wanted sheltered housing to replace it). Certainly the outside had become an eyesore through neglect and fly-posting but the government accepted English Heritage's recommendation that the Rex should remain on the register of listed properties. This encouraged the Friends of the Rex to seek to acquire the building for use as a cinema or community centre. Film critic Barry Norman became honorary president of the Save the Rex campaign. As still nothing happened, the Rex became one of fifty-one post-1914 structures highlighted in the Twentieth Century Society's first 'Buildings at Risk' report in 1998.

An application by the Friends of the Rex to the National Lottery Fund to purchase and restore the cinema was turned down, but the Friends then formed the Rex Film and Arts Centre Trust with the aim of raising funds from elsewhere to purchase the building. In March 1999, a group of independent business consultants produced a report for a film-based arts centre: this called for a 472-seat cinema in the existing auditorium with two 260-seat cinemas above, a tiered car park, a bar, café, restaurant and other leisure facilities. A rival scheme proposed a swimming pool in the auditorium area with thirty-seven flats around it.

A coach party of Cinema Theatre Association members turned up outside the Rex on 25 September 1999 to lend support to the Trust but was not able to gain access to the inside of the building. New plans surfaced for a pub in the foyer, with thirty-seven flats elsewhere (still around a

swimming pool?). The Trust staged a Rex Film Night at the Town Hall on 12 November when a film made in 1988 of the Rex's closure called *The Last House* was shown.

There was concern when a developer claimed that the building had fallen into a perilous state but it was reported that the Trust was prevented from entering the building to check on its condition. Nicholas King Homes proposed building flats around a 600-seat cinema in the existing auditorium which would be restored from the proceeds of selling the flats and which could be operated by the Trust. However, the Trust proposed a multi-purpose arts venue with a

The auditorium of the Rex Berkhamsted in 1938.

three-screen cinema, gaining support from broadcaster (and later British Film Institute Chair) Joan Bakewell, and actors Hugh Grant, Hayley Mills and Ian Richardson, but the Council was worried that the Trust's proposal for three cinemas would exacerbate existing parking problems in the area.

In December 2000, both schemes were reported to have received planning permission but it was the Nicholas King Homes one which went ahead. The foyer was dramatically repainted in red and black with gold highlighting of the scalloped edges of the stepped ceiling recess to serve temporarily, from February 2002, as a sales office for the flats (to be known as The Rex Apartments) being built within the framework of the former parade of shops and behind the auditorium in the old car park with ground floor parking space. The foyer has gained a new chandelier, not in the original style, while the mirrors on the stairs have either been refurbished or recreated.

To the company's credit, it has taken the art deco aspects of the cinema as an inspiration for the design of the thirty-two one- and two-bedroom flats with bathrooms in the style of a 1930s star's dressing room, maple-veneered doors and chrome iron-mongery, and scallop-shaped light fittings in communal hallways. However, once its marketing function has ceased, the foyer has been leased for use as a Fish! restaurant, part of an up-market sea-food chain. The steps that once led to the stalls will now lead only to kitchens. Reaching the auditorium through its imposing entrance and spectacular foyer was an integral part of the cinema-going experience offered by the Rex and it is an appalling decision to break up the unity of the original scheme in this way and to deflect patrons into using a new entrance down the side of the building. One can only hope that the foyer space proves commercially unviable and becomes directly linked to the cinema again at some future date. It will be interesting also to see whether the Rex's name will be displayed with its old prominence and where the restaurant will place its signage.

The auditorium area has been leased to James Hannaway and is expected to re-open during November 2002. Nicholas King Homes has restored the building to its original single screen condition while the cinema operator is installing the projection equipment, carpet and seats. According to a statement issued by Mr Hannaway, "There will be one screen, showing some of the latest films, alongside a programme of art-house/retro/genre/fringe/classic films throughout the year. Viewing will be from the permanent balcony (the original circle), with flexible cabaret seating in the stalls area downstairs. Wheelchair access will be into the stalls. Reserved spaces downstairs will be at tables with usher/bar service available throughout the film/performance. There will be two bars, one in the foyer upstairs, the other under the balcony downstairs. Each will carry a good wine list, and a selection of the best coffees, ices, juices and international drinks. There will be no fruit machines or popcorn. Film soundtracks will greet the audience as they gather in the foyer and the auditorium. On occasions musicians will play in both arenas. The stalls area will accommodate non-film activities and events which need good standing/banqueting/concert space. The film programme will run (initially) from Thursday to Sunday, including matinées and early screenings for children and teenagers. Monday to Wednesday will be reserved for other activities, some arts-based, other commercial. Depending on demand and seasonal variations, the following activities are envisaged: conferences and exhibitions; education (packages for schools); commercial/corporate functions; casting and professional rehearsals; location site for Film-Link, Leavesden Studios; children's holiday activities; film-based workshops/projects; 'four-wall' partnerships (hire of whole cinema space for public/private showings not organised or financed by the Rex); concerts, performances, readings, lectures, party showings, special events."

This ambitious scheme promises to

make the Rex the outstanding place to experience the traditional cinemagoing experience in Hertfordshire and a very rare example of a restored 1930s auditorium in its original use. Every reader of this book should make an effort to support it.

BISHOP'S STORTFORD

Saturday 10 February 1912

Cinema / Phoenix

1 South Street

The Cinema was an adaptation of the former PSA Hall, originally built as a Methodist chapel in 1866 and closed in 1903. A new colonnade-style frontage was erected, linoleum and carpet were laid in the passageways, and around 400 seats

The Bishop's Stortford Cinema as it originally looked. (Courtesy of Kevin S. Wheelan.)

The Bishop's Stortford Cinema, probably around 1920. (Courtesy of Kevin S. Wheelan.)

The Bishop's Stortford Cinema closed after the 1932 fire. The posters advertise films at the Regent and Sawbridgeworth Cinema, both under the same management. (Courtesy of Kevin S. Wheelan.)

were installed – plush red 'tip-ups' on the sloping floor of the gallery at the rear and about 200 seats that did not tip up for the cheaper front section. The picture was by rear projection from a box situated well behind the screen. The first manager, Alfred J. Hatrick, within a year became managing director of the Hoddesdon Cinema Company which opened the Cinema there.

In 1914, the auditorium of the Bishop's Stortford Cinema was enlarged to seat 100

The Bishop's Stortford Cinema as the Phoenix, September 1935.

more with a larger stage. It re-opened on 15 August, at which time a second projector was brought into use. In October 1916, the Cinema was taken over by Ernest E. Smith who had previously opened a cinema in Saffron Walden. In 1919, a balcony was added and re-opening took place on 9 November. Local historian Dorothy Cleal remembers the Phoenix as have "much fading red plush and peeling stucco in its later days, usually showing the older films and 'B' pictures. It was the scene of my first cinema experience, which must have been 1928/9 – *The Gold Rush* – Charlie Chaplin, of course. My father had to take me out because the sight of Charlie eating his boot brought on a screaming fit."

Rear projection may have been changed when talkies arrived with *The Love Parade*, shown from 9 February 1931. The Cinema closed as a result of serious fire damage in March 1932.

It was decided to build a new picture house from the ashes of the old and give it the appropriate name of the Phoenix. Opening took place on 23 September 1935 with Grace Moore in *One Night of Love*.

There were some 600 seats including double seats for courting couples. The Phoenix was of secondary importance to the Regent and, when the town could no longer support two cinemas, it closed on 3 May 1958 with a routine Hollywood picture, *Crime in the Streets*. A Tesco Home 'n' Wear store replaced it and this had closed by 1983. It became a branch of W. H. Smith, which continues to conduct business there in early 2002.

Monday 25 March 1912

Empire Picture Palace

20 South Street

Purpose-built between the fire station and the Workmen's Club to plans of Houston and Houston by builders J. L. Glasscock for its joint proprietors, F. A. Dando and C. E. A. Gilbert, the Empire had its screen by the front entrance and its projection box at the back of the site where there was also a shed for leaving bicycles. The hall measured 67ft by 30ft. Its floor had a slope of 1 in 10 and accommodated 500.

The last advertised programme is for 23 April 1914 when, besides films, there was the "return engagement of Miss Mabel Thomas – comedienne, dancer and club juggler", a reminder that variety was usually mixed with films at that time. However, as Ernest E. Smith is said to have paid the Empire £1 per week to stop showing films after he took over the rival Cinema, it would seem to have been open at least until late 1916. In 1985, there was a Burton store at 20 South Street, which has been subdivided to include Dorothy Perkins in early 2002.

The Empire Picture Palace at Bishop's Stortford, circa 1912. (Courtesy of Philip Yaxley.)

Monday 9 November 1931

Regent / Granada

11 South Street

Ernest E. Smith realised the town needed a larger, more modern cinema and, if he had not provided it, some other entrepreneur would certainly have stepped in. Thus, besides operating the town's Cinema (later Phoenix) and the nearby Sawbridgeworth Cinema, Mr Smith added the Regent, which was designed for him by E.M. Allan-Hallett and reputedly had 999 seats to avoid taxes

The Regent Bishop's Stortford on 23 September 1965, prior to modernisation by new owners Granada.

which became payable on 1,000 or more. It opened with the spectacular *Trader Horn*. Mr Smith's sons, G. P. A. (Percy) and Eric, helped run the cinemas and in 1983 Eric Smith recalled in the *Herts and Essex Observer* that the Regent kept a stock of umbrellas for patrons to borrow if it was raining as they left. He also remembered an amusing publicity stunt when *The Invisible Man* was shown in 1934. A white rod was put in a barrel outside the Regent with a notice reading: "The Invisible Man will climb this pole at 3pm". Sure enough, a crowd gathered... Eric Smith also claimed that the blue, red and white neon display on the front of the Regent was the largest in the Eastern Counties.

The Regent was so successful that a private bus company used to adjust its schedules to pick up audiences as they left after the evening shows.

Because of the Quaker beliefs of the Smith brothers, the Regent never opened on Sundays, other than for charity shows during the war years. The Smiths also refused to show X certificate films after the adults-only category was introduced in 1950. "We did not show 'X' films or horror films – those are the films that destroyed what used to be good family entertainment," recalled Eric Smith in 1983. "We never had any vandalism – no seats were ripped or damaged. We always provided what the public wanted." These attitudes increasingly limited the Regent's appeal and must have made it look old-fashioned to the

View across the balcony at the Regent Bishop's Stortford, taken 23 September 1965.

younger element which became the core cinema audience, especially when many box-office hits in the X category never played Bishop's Stortford. Afternoon performances were dropped, except for Saturdays. There was no children's show on Saturday mornings. The Regent seemed in serious decline, yet the town was large enough to support a cinema more in tune with modern tastes and habits, Sunday being one of the busiest days for cinemagoing.

Certainly the cinema's potential was evident to the Granada circuit which took over the property from 23 August 1965. *Mary Poppins* broke the cinema's takings record just after Granada took over but the long-serving staff did not readily adapt to Granada's style of management, especially as one of the Smiths lived in a flat opposite and kept dropping in to remind them of the "old days". Granada had to change managers twice in the first year to get its way. Matinées were resumed; a Granadiers Saturday morning club began on 16 October 1965; Sunday revival double-bills commenced on 26 July 1966. Sex and horror films with X certificates became frequent, along with one-

day bookings of ballet, opera and Shakespeare films.

Granada soon commissioned its regular architects, George Coles and Partners, a leading practice in cinema work, to draw up a renovation scheme. This was carried out – the cinema remained open, except for the cancellation of ten matinée performances, and re-opened renamed the Granada on Monday 30 January 1967 under a live-wire manager, Brian Gauntlett, with a gala screening of *My Fair Lady* attended by a cluster of show-biz personalities and the heads of many film distribution companies. The original wide arched entrance had been filled in with three sets of new doors and a Granada shop serving both patrons from the foyer and passers-by from an entrance on the street. This sold sweets, cigarettes, newspapers and magazines. The interior was spruced up with new curtains in front of the screen and two rows of seats removed, leaving 600 seats in the stalls and 260 in the balcony.

In December 1967, the Granada played a Japanese film, *Onibaba*, which had been banned by the British Board of Film Censors for its sex and horror content. This was supported by *Nudist Paradise*. In the book *The Granada Theatres* (1998), Gauntlett recalled: "By November 1967, only eighteen city and county councils had granted permission for *Onibaba* to be screened in their licensing areas. This figure included Hertfordshire County Council, which covered the Granada Bishop's Stortford, but excluded Essex County Council. This meant the film could not be screened at the Odeon Harlow, only seven miles away. I quickly seized on the opportunity to capture adult Harlow cinemagoers away from their local cinema. Such was the

The Regent lost its arched entrance to modern doors and a sweet shop when it became the Granada. Photograph taken 18 February 1967.

The Regent Bishop's Stortford in 1930s. (Courtesy of Kevin S. Wheelan.)

relationship between Granada and [the film's distributor] Orb that [its managing director] Nat Miller agreed with me to equally share all costs of advertising expenditure without further detail or limit. A giant publicity and press campaign was organised, which attracted patrons from as far away as Southend and Bedford. The cinema broke its Sunday box-office record and the film produced capacity evening business throughout the week."

In the 1970s, Granada began converting its larger buildings into three-screen cinemas or transferring them to bingo operation. The company became more interested in bingo than cinema and decided that the Bishop's Stortford Granada would be more profitable as a

bingo hall. Permission was first sought for change of use in the spring of 1973. There was considerable opposition to the proposed loss of the town's only cinema and it took more than two years and an appeal to the Minister of the Environment before permission for bingo was finally obtained. The cinema closed on Saturday 22 January 1977 after the final performance of *Night of the Grizzly*. Granada Bingo soon followed but does not seem to have been as successful as anticipated. At any rate, in late 1982 Marks and Spencer acquired the building and adjacent shops for the site of a new store. Demolition was completed in September 1983 and work began on the new building the following month. Marks and Spencer still occupy the site in 2002 and no sign remains of any of the three cinemas that were built so close to each other in narrow South Street.

An attempt was made from Thursday 30 August 1979 to establish a small video cinema at the Triad Leisure Centre in Southmill Road, but this was short-lived and Bishop's Stortford would remain in the dark as far as big-screen entertainment was concerned for over twenty years.

Wednesday 6 and Friday 8 December 2000

Cineworld

Anchor Street

C inema returned to Bishop's Stortford in a substantial way as part of the Anchor Street leisure centre development by Citygrove Leisure. The Cineworld chain, which already operated the multiplex at Stevenage among others, leased the upper area designated for cinema use, although it provided far fewer screens than their other sites. The cinema was officially opened by the Mayor of Bishop's Stortford at a private party on a Wednesday to which all those involved in the cinema were invited. The foyer was decked out for the occasion as a tropical casino with palm trees and various film-star lookalikes such as a Jack Nicholson mingled with the guests while a Frank Sinatra was among those providing the cabaret. The public were admitted two days later.

It was on the edge of the city centre, half-hidden behind a separate sports centre building, with a narrow access road and no car parking facilities of its own. Dominating the entrance is a large McDonalds, and the six-screen Cineworld

The exit staircase at the entrance to the Cineworld Bishop's Stortford. (Courtesy of Cine-UK.)

on the upper floor is reached by an escalator at the back. There is a landing at the top with the main Cineworld sign mounted above it. A staircase extends alongside the escalator for exiting the cinema and the area has a glazed, curving frontage extending to ground level through which the brightly illuminated name sign can be seen from the town centre across the River Stort immediately outside. Another Cineworld sign is displayed by the outer entrance.

As usual in a multiplex, the most spectacular area is the foyer. Here it forms a lofty space dominated by a suspended circular bank of video monitors showing

The spacious foyer of the Cineworld Bishop's Stortford with the cactus representation of westerns half visible at the left. (Courtesy of Cine-UK.)

trailers and other publicity material, fringed at a distance by a curious arrangement of two semi-transparent screens that curve around the central feature. The usual ticket office and concession counter are accompanied by a pick 'n' mix corner and a video games area half concealed behind a wall. An engaging decorative touch around the upper walls is the symbolic display of the various film genres with a banana skin representing comedy, a skull representing horror, etc.

This Cineworld was Cine-UK's twentieth UK multiplex and its second in Hertfordshire after Stevenage. With only six auditoria, it had the minimum size to qualify as a multiplex. The seating figures are 299, 104, 160, 259, 230 and 185 – a total of 1,237 (other Cineworld multiplexes have at least eight screens). Accessed from a corridor extending from the far corner of the foyer and served by a single lengthy projection suite above, all the auditoria have stadium seating to ensure a clear view of the screen. Although a slightly risky venture in that the local cinemagoing habit had to be revived after twenty years, the multiplex has performed creditably from the very start, denting attendances at the cinemas in Harlow.

BOREHAMWOOD

1914

Gem

1 Station Road
(originally Gasworks Lane)

Standing outside Elstree and Borehamwood railway station, the present day Eau de Toilette flower shop hardly suggests a former cinema. In fact, the building started life as a Baptist chapel in 1894. The Baptists moved to Shenley Road in 1911 and the building was taken over and adapted into the Gem cinema by the Neptune Film Company which had built a studio in early 1914 in the area. Reputedly seating a maximum of 150 squeezed onto wooden benches, it may have served as a private viewing theatre for the company as well as a public cinema in the evenings, showing Neptune's productions and others. Charging admission prices of 1d, 2d and 3d, it apparently claimed to be the smallest cinema in the world. The Neptune company ceased production and the studio passed to new owners in 1917. Whether the cinema closed at this time has not been established.

A vivid reminiscence of the Gem was provided by F. C. Hart in an article for the 'Down Memory Lane' section of the *Boreham Wood Post* in 1981 (date unknown) when the building had become a public convenience:

"I reflected with nostalgia that, where trap No. 2 in the gents' now stands, was the exact spot upon which stood the honky-tonk piano. I could once more hear the pianist hammering out the old and familiar diddle-diddle-dum, diddle-diddle-dum, ter-dumpty, to add excitement to the chase. It was here, in the days of my youth, that I thrilled to the escapades of Edie Polo, Pola Negri, Pearl White, Bill Anderson the cowboy and the Keystone Cops. What wonderful times they were! Owing to the bad quality of the film in those days and the constant friction of bad projection, every episode appeared to be enacted in a torrential rainstorm. But what did we care as long as the picture moved. Mind you, in seeking such entertainment we suffered many hazards. I cannot remember a single performance being given without something going wrong. And, of course, it was not to be wondered at, for there was no electricity and the projector was illuminated by what was called a limelight. Roughly speaking, the system was produced by the action of an oxyhydrogen flame played upon a ball of lime – until the bottle of hydrogen gas ran out, usually halfway through the performance. There would then be a pause of some twenty minutes, while the proprietor and the projectionist made a frenzied dash over the fence to the railway station to see if a new bottle of gas had arrived by a late passenger train. If it had, all well and good. But if it had not, we the audience were invited by the panting proprietor to receive our money back at the paybox on our way out.

"The projector was hand-operated and likewise the film re-winder. The projector handle had to be turned with even continuity in order to keep the uniformity of the picture action – if you see what I mean. The operator, having laboriously churned through part one, was compelled by nature to take a rest in order to ease his aching arm and restore his personal comfort. Part two usually appeared on the screen either upside down, backwards or in two half frames. It would be several minutes before the operator's attention was drawn to the fact that all was not well, by cat-calls, boos and whistles from an unappreciative audience…. The operator had other worries on his hands, or rather on his feet. His assistant could never seem to catch up with the rewinding of the film, which lay in festoons upon the floor. Although the projection room was solidly built of brick, the risk of fire was always in my mind.

"We suffered the glorious agony of our weekly visit to the pictures for some years and then the proprietor had a brilliant idea. He bought an old car engine and an antiquated electric generator and thus converted the projector to electric power. We were now getting much more for our money – the film, the piano, and all accompanied by the whine of the genera-tor and the thump-thump of the engine revving like mad in an effort to produce sufficient light. Unfortunately, the engine was prone to breakdowns and, on occa-sions, in the middle of an exciting episode, you would hear the thumping die down, and of course, the picture automatically died with it… If possible, the engine was repaired while we sat in the dark listening to an alleged recital given by the pianist. After a pause vary-ing from five to twenty-five minutes, we would hear the engine begin to pick up and the picture re-appeared …"

Before the building became a public convenience, it was used by the Council as an office for collecting rates and rents. When demolition was proposed in 1996, its earlier cinematic use was recalled in an illustrated story in *The Times* (7 July). It stood unused until 1998 when it became the Eau de Toilette flower shop. The main entrance is the former doorway to the Ladies, retaining the old iron gate, and there are plenty of signs of its use as a public toilet in the cisterns and pull chains and numbered cubicle doors but, not surprisingly, there is no evidence that it was ever a cinema. The owners display a short history of the building on an inside wall near the entrance.

Monday 30 March 1936

Studio / Studio 70

231 Shenley Road
(corner of Brook Road)

The first proposal to build a large, modern cinema in Shenley Road was put forward in February 1935 when plans were submitted to Barnet Rural Council by Tudor Cinemas (Elstree), headed by one E. G. Whiting. The 1,200-seat cinema, to be called the Tudor, would be com-pletely in the style of that period with an 'olde English' garden in front, a Tudor house frontage, a baronial hall-style of foyer, and staff dressed in costume. At a time when streamlined art deco was taking hold, a fanciful scheme of this kind was rather out of date – although draw-ings suggest that it would have been elab-orate and thorough, and it might have made a worthy counterpart to some earlier cinemas like the Gaumont Palace (now Odeon) Salisbury and Beaufort Birmingham (demolished) which made very attractive use of a Tudor theme. In any case, the plans were rejected in February 1935, apparently because coun-cillors believed the scheme was too large for the area.

The smaller and far more prosaic Studio that was built shortly afterwards in

Shenley Road seated 820. Designed by E. B. Parkinson for the Fletcher-Barnet syndicate, it was identical to the Studio (later Orion) Hassocks, West Sussex, which opened over two years later. Parkinson was also the architect of cinemas at Hatfield and Royston in Hertfordshire.

Although the Studio was in Borehamwood, at the northern end of the main shopping street, it advertised itself as the Studio Elstree. While Elstree village is two miles away, the area as a whole is often known as Elstree and the major film and television production complex with its entrance block almost opposite the cinema has always been known as Elstree Studios.

The Studio cinema was taken over by the S & K circuit around September 1937 and generally played films a week or more after St Albans. It had no difficulty performing well during the boom years of cinemagoing in the 1940s and 1950s. John Brierley worked there during the late 1950s: "In the projection box there was just the chief and myself, with a part-time projectionist coming in at 6pm four days a week. On the day one of us was off, the other worked by himself. The screen masking [the black edge] was opened by hand – so, when we had a CinemaScope trailer or feature, we would have to shut down the projector and race downstairs to the stage to alter the masking, and then back up again to continue. On many occasions I had the warning 'the council was in' [for a licensing inspection] but for some reason they never got beyond the manager's office. The council inspectors in the Middlesex area, about every two months, would check that every exit and fire exit was clear, there was adequate staff on duty inside the auditorium and projection

The Studio Elstree (Borehamwood), circa 1964. (Courtesy of Kevin S. Wheelan.)

area, and check for any fire risk. I have known them to arrive in the morning and check every seat to make sure it would go back into the upright position. They had the authority to close a cinema. Yet in Hertfordshire, they were more relaxed, as on many occasions there was only one of us on duty in the box.

"Under the stage at the Studio cinema

The auditorium of the Studio Elstree (Borehamwood) at opening in 1936. The curtains have been opened to display the round-cornered screen in the dimensions that were standard before wide screens. (Author's collection, courtesy of T. J. Braybon and John Fernee.)

*The new entrance and cladding hiding the old
frontage for the rebranding of the Studio Elstree
(Borehamwood) as the Studio 70 in 1966. (Courtesy
of Kevin S. Wheelan.)*

*A poor quality image of the modernised interior of
the Studio 70 Elstree (Borehamwood) with festoon
curtains to enable to maximum width of wide screen
and cladding over the side walls*

was a massive popcorn machine which
had come from America for Douglas
Fairbanks Jr when filming in Elstree and
was then given to the cinema. I don't
know if it was ever used. From the roof we
had a view of the countryside: in one field
stood a large castle, used for the film
Knights of the Round Table. Another night,
one of the fields was full of bonfires as
they were filming *Zulu*. And I remember
watching Cliff Richard filming outside the
gates of the studios."

The first major alterations occurred in
1966 when the Studio closed for a three-
month modernisation scheme drawn up
by architect George Beech. The old
frontage disappeared behind a wall of
fibreglass. A huge illuminated panel was
erected to advertise the current programme. Inside, a steeper rake was introduced in both stalls and circle to improve
sightlines, seats were set in a curve with
improved spacing between rows, and a
modern decor was provided. Finally, the
cinema was re-named the Studio 70 for its
gala re-opening with a pre-release showing of *Carry On Cowboy* on Saturday 2
April. There were now 710 seats. The Kalee
projectors, dating from 1944, were
retained.

By 1980, the cinema had dropped
weekday matinées and was bothered by
unruly behaviour in the evenings, refusing
admittance after 7pm to unaccompanied
youngsters under 16 years of age. EMI,
which had taken over the S & K circuit, put
the Studio 70 up for sale. On 31 January of
that year plans were submitted to replace
the cinema with a DIY store and offices.
These and revised plans put forward by a
development company were rejected by
the planning authorities. When three peti-
tions containing 3,000 signatures were
sent to the area's recreation and amenities
committee in May 1980, EMI replied that
less than two per cent of the local population supported the cinema but it might
stay open if a guarantee against losses was
offered. By May 1981, the site had been

sold. The cinema's final programme was a double-bill of *Stir Crazy* and *California Suite* that ended its run on Saturday 6 June 1981. The building was demolished in December 1981 although its large illuminated signboard was bought for the Civic Hall on Elstree Way where films were already being regularly shown in the 662-seat auditorium. (This later became the Hertsmere Centre and The Venue before being demolished in October 1997 for a new theatre that was never built.) The Studio cinema's site is occupied by part of two office blocks, which in 2002 are called Isopad House and (behind) Hertsmere House.

When the Elstree film studios were bought by Brent Walker in 1988, planning permission was granted for a multiplex cinema on the front two acres of the 13-acre site but, after Hertsmere Council compulsorily purchased the lot, it deliberately ruled out any such development by refusing to allow the essential car parking space because it would reduce the area available for film-making facilities, which had already been severely reduced by the construction of a Tesco superstore. (In fact, the council did discuss the construction of a 150-seat IMAX cinema to accompany proposals for production offices for the IMAX company.)

The entrance to the Omniplex Cinemas at Borehamwood within the leisure centre with the box office to the right. (Photograph by Allen Eyles.)

became vacant when Tesco built a new store on part of the Elstree Studios site. The developer, Oppenheims, provided space for a ground-floor 630-seat four-screen miniplex along with a bowling alley, pool hall, bar and parking space for 240 cars. The entertainment centre was originally scheduled to open in March 1997. Three parties were interested in showing films there, including ABC Cinemas, but the space was eventually leased to a new local company, Senior Screens, formed by the Senior family from Elstree that included a veteran film production and distribution executive, Julian Senior.

The Cinema opened on Tuesday 19 January 1999 as the first section of the Metropolis Centre to be completed, with the bowling alley and a fitness centre announced to follow in the early spring. There was an invited audience for a special advance showing of the Tom Hanks/Meg Ryan romantic comedy *You've Got Mail* on two screens, and celebrities on hand included Jenny Agutter, Susan George, film critic Barry Norman and

*Tuesday 19 and
Friday 22 January 1999*

The Cinema / Omniplex

Metropolis Centre (now The Point),
84 Shenley Road

This was part of a £4 million redevelopment of the former Tesco supermarket in the centre of Borehamwood which two stars from *EastEnders*. The general public had to wait until the following Friday when three current releases – *Little Voice, Enemy of the State* and *Star Trek Insurrection* – were offered as the main attractions along with the new *Practical Magic*. The four auditoria seated 180, 144, 111 and 108. The programming policy also included a regular classic matinée initiated by *It's a Wonderful Life* and a Saturday and Sunday morning children's club which opened with *Small Soldiers*.

For some reason, perhaps linked to the general response to the Metropolis Centre, the Cinema did not catch on. Business was so poor that it was forced to close less than two years later on Thursday 7 September 2000, immediately after the collapse of a proposed take-over by Leisure Box, the company operating the bowling alley at the Metropolis Centre. *The Borehamwood and Elstree Times* noted that, although the Cinema has been popular with children and staged promotions and premières, it had failed to attract enough adult cinemagoers. Julian Senior was quoted as saying: "We put a huge amount of effort into providing the best cinema we could afford to build in Borehamwood. We did everything we could, but unfortunately not enough people turned up ... apart from a few big blockbuster films."

The owners of the leisure centre looked for another operator and discussions were taking place with two companies in mid-2001. These were resolved when the largest cinema operator in Ireland, Ward-Anderson, took over the site for its first outlet in mainland Britain. The cinemas had been stripped out and the new lessees installed larger screens than those that had been there before, plus new carpet, seating, sound system and projection equipment. The positioning of aisles and general seating configuration was altered and the four auditoria now seated 193, 157, 121 and 119 – 47 more seats than previously. A robust use of red and blue replaced the lighter colours of the original decorative scheme.

The cinemas were re-opened using Ward-Anderson's customary Omniplex name on Friday 15 February 2002, offering *Ocean's Eleven, Monsters Inc., Lord of the Rings, Vanilla Sky* and several other films, with late night shows on Fridays and Saturdays. Outside of school holidays, the cinemas normally start up around 4pm on weekdays. The leisure centre has been renamed The Point to give it a fresh start. A restaurant space opposite the cinema awaited a new tenant in March 2002 but a bowling alley, bar and health club were operative.

BUNTINGFORD

Friday 12 December 1913

Picturedrome

Station Road

Before a Mr Marshall opened his full-time Picturedrome, there had been film performances at the annual Buntingford Show in a marquee or other temporary structure. Mr Marshall had brought his Hippodrome here, a travelling circus that performed in a tent in a field (perhaps for the annual Show). His Picturedrome appears to have petered out after 1916. It seems likely that this was in fact the name used for shows presented at the Benson Hall (see below) rather than in some other building.

Friday 8 September 1933

Buntingford Cinema / Benson Hall Cinema / Cosy

Station Road

The Benson Hall was part of the Catholic church complex erected as a memorial to R. H. Benson during the First World War. It was used for weekly film shows from early on and season tickets at reduced prices were issued. This use ceased during the 1920s.

On 8 September 1933, the Buntingford Cinema opened in the same hall with new sound apparatus, showing Laurel and Hardy in *Pack up your Troubles* and two of the Barrymores in *Arsene Lupin*. It could seat 280 including a small gallery that housed the projection equipment. The floor was always flat rather than raked. Films were then shown only on Fridays and Saturdays. It was one of several part-time cinemas operated by E. H. Rockett (others were at Ashwell, Redbourn and Knebworth). Shows were discontinued around March 1934.

On 7 September 1934 the Benson Hall Cinema was launched here under new management with more new talking apparatus, but the screen apparently went dark again in January 1935.

The Cosy Buntingford, "the Little House with the Big Reputation", opened here in February 1936 with one programme on Mondays and Wednesdays and another on Thursdays and Saturdays. It was run by A. E. Gore's Touring Talking Picture Company of King's Lynn and he also operated a Cosy at Redbourn. It had the obscure Morrison sound system. Between 13 and 30 July 1936 the Cosy shut for redecoration and alterations that included closing off the gallery to turn it into a projection box. With 200 seats, it then (or soon after) ran full-time (two changes weekly) except for Sundays (which presumably would not have been permitted by the church landlords). Local historian Philip Plumb has recalled: "A children's matinée was instituted – seats 3d (the front) and 6d (at the back). Tickets qualified for a free draw for a bar of chocolate and those paying sixpence got two dips – once I won both times. During the Second World War the Cosy was well patronised by not only the local people but soldiers from the large REME workshop at the south end of Buntingford."

The last proprietor, from the early 1950s, was a local man, Tom Cooper. By now the Cosy had a leading sound system, B.T.H. (British Thomson-Houston). The cinema was obscured from sight on the main road by the small fire station built in front of the Benson Hall in 1931. Its most conspicuous advertising was a poster outside the sweet

The Cosy Buntingford in the 1950s. (The Cinema Museum.)

shop next to the garage on the other side of the main road. The Cosy bowed to the changes in leisure habits by closing in August 1958.

Over the years it had also served as an occasional live theatre – the Buntingford Dramatic Society presented Christmas pantomimes on the 12ft deep stage, using the two dressing rooms.

After remaining empty a few years, the hall was leased by an engineering firm and it became the Riverside Works of Keith Building Services. Externally, it had hardly altered since it was first built.

CHESHUNT

Late 1913
Cinema / Kozy / Central
College Road

T he Cinema was an adaptation of St Mary's Hall, built as a public hall in 1862 and used for concerts, poetry readings, magic lantern shows, etc. It was Captain Cecil Clayton who first introduced moving pictures with one-night presentations when one penny was charged to sit on wooden benches. A certain Mr Cluff opened it as a full-time cinema, then quickly sold it in February 1914 to the Hoddesdon Cinema Company. It had about 300 seats.

Around 1928 it took the name Kozy. When the Regent at nearby Waltham Cross closed for thorough modernisation, the Kozy decided that it had to follow suit. It shut after 12 September 1931 for "rebuilding, reseating and the installation of the latest talkie apparatus. The alterations include the erection of a spacious balcony". Under the new name of the Central, it re-opened on Thursday 29 October 1931 with a three-day run of the former Aldwych farce *Plunder*. With its new balcony, the Central had around 400 seats.

In 1933 E. J. 'Chips' Carpenter, who had been manager of the Castle Hertford, took over and remained as proprietor and manager until the Central's closure when he was seventy-eight years old.

In the 1930s there was considerable interest in building a new cinema on Turners Hill where it meets the High Street on a site almost facing Church Lane. Plans for a Royal cinema (architect: Bertie Crewe) for F. J. Partner & Company were submitted in July 1935; then came plans by Robert Cromie for a Ritz in February 1937; and finally Pavilion Cinemas (which built the Welwyn Pavilion) proposed a 900-seat single-floor building in January 1938, designed by J. Edmund Farrell. Fortunately for 'Chips' Carpenter, opposition never came.

It was the nationwide decline in attendances, aggravated by the delay in securing the big films (which always played at the larger cinemas in Waltham Cross first), that eventually forced Mr Carpenter to close. The last film show on Saturday 28 February 1959 consisted of *6.5 Special* plus *Shake, Rattle and Rock*. The building was demolished some time after 1965. Its site was taken over by a new Lloyds Bank in the Manorcroft Parade redevelopment, and Lloyds are still there in early 2002.

The Central Cheshunt, circa 1958.

ELSTREE

See BOREHAMWOOD

HARPENDEN

Wednesday 14 May 1913

White Palace / Victoria Theatre

Leyton Road/Amenbury Lane

T he White Palace lived up to its name with a predominantly white frontage relieved by red brick; it was designed by Montie J. Thorpe, an architect in the practice of Henry F. Mence in St Albans, for the White Palace Syndicate headed by A. Clements, a man from London who had invested his savings in the scheme.

Publicity stunt for the film Carnival *at the White Palace Harpenden, circa 1921. (Courtesy of Eric Brandreth.)*

There were 450 seats, including twenty-five in a gallery at the right-hand side of the screen where the piano for accompanying the silent films was originally located. Only the best seats were 'tip-ups'. There was one box at the back. The first pianist was the writer Ursula Bloom, who has provided vivid accounts of her eighteen months there in various books of autobiography: *Mistress of None* (1933), *Youth at the Gate* (1959), *A Roof and Four Walls* (1967) and *Life is no Fairy Tale* (1976).

The gallery provided an excellent vantage point for seeing the screen but the vibration and echo from the roof made it unsuitable for the piano which was moved after two days to behind a curtain in front of the screen: there Miss Bloom not only suffered from a crick in the neck looking up at the picture but also from attempts by youths in the audience to pinch her bottom through the curtains! She has also recalled that the dynamo kept failing during the first week and money had to be refunded twice. She was required to play the piano from 6pm to 10.30pm with about two-and-a-half minutes rest every half-hour between the short films that then made up the pro-

Architect's drawing of the front elevation of the White Palace Harpenden.

grammes (feature-length films were only just being introduced). In addition, there were matinées to be played on Wednesdays and Saturdays from 2.30pm to 5pm. For all her work, Miss Bloom was paid thirty shillings a week.

When war broke out, the male staff were called up and Ursula Bloom became manager as well as pianist for a short time before leaving. "The coming of the war in the cinema world was intensely thrilling," she wrote in 1933. "Those first telegrams, those extra editions, the latest news flashed on the screen. I played patriotic airs until my hands nearly dropped off. I used to print with a pin on smoked slides, announcing the news from the front. I had always been good at printing, and my latent faculty for journalism produced some stirring slides..."

Mr Clements had little idea about booking films but Miss Bloom remembers accompanying successful engagements of full-length epics like *Les Miserables* and *Quo Vadis?* The White Palace soon passed to other hands and from around 1917 was run by Captain F. A. Webb, an Australian whose rank had been reached in the Mounted Police Down Under and who had shown films in Melbourne and around Australia before coming to Britain. He had converted a barn at Leighton Buzzard into that town's first cinema, the Old Vic, and he renamed the White Palace – it became the Victoria Theatre after his home state in Australia. Captain Webb sold the cinema to a Mr and Mrs Howard circa 1931 and they installed the British Acoustic sound system. Margaret Howard soon decided that the building was no longer adequate and closed it in 1933 when she opened the Regent.

From 1935, the building was used by clothing manufacturers – George E. Bevins (knitted goods) was succeeded in 1941 by S. Newman (ladies' underwear) who gave way in October 1953 to L. S. and J. Sussman. An engineering concern was using the premises by 1970, and they have been occupied in recent years by the Hunton Bridge Engineering Company, retaining their old cinema name by being known as the Victoria Works. A row of shops with flats above has been built in front of the cinema on Leyton Road but the end of the auditorium can still be seen on Amenbury Lane.

Friday 26 May 1933

Regent / State

Leyton Road, near Church Green

Margaret Howard acquired the old Methodist chapel and had it converted into a 410-seat cinema with another white frontage that was outlined in red, green and blue neon. The Regent was equipped with the reliable B.T.H. sound system and opened with an all-British programme. It was soon

leased by J. C. Southgate who then bought it early in 1936.

Sunday opening came late to Harpenden. When a poll was held on Saturday 6 December 1947 over whether cinemas should be allowed to open on that day, 29 per cent of the electorate turned out to vote. The result was 1,753 for and 1,182 against. The Regent's first Sunday show followed on 15 February 1948 after the necessary licences had been issued. *Song of the Open Road* was shown, supported by *Don't Hook Now*. More than a thousand people attended the day's showings at the town's two cinemas.

In later years, the Regent was owned by F. S. Norris and run as a repertory cinema since its small size and independent ownership prevented it from obtaining any major new films on first release. In September and October 1952 Mr Norris turned the slack first half of the week over to a season of specialised films – operas, French pictures like *La Belle et la Bête*, off beat Hollywood productions like José Ferrer's *Cyrano de Bergerac*. But it was soon back to more basic fare, catering particularly to teenagers with lower prices than the rival Embassy, and doing its best business on Sundays.

The Regent adopted sexy foreign films in 1959 and introduced a change of name – "State for adult entertainment" – to mark the change of policy. Advertising in the local press soon largely disappeared but the last programme seems to have been a highly respectable French picture *Summer Manoeuvres*, supported even more respectably by Chaplin's *The Pilgrim*, for the week ending 19 September 1959. The State closed "for redecoration" but when it re-opened it was as the furniture department of the adjacent Anscombe's store (which had supplied the draperies and carpets when it started in 1933). It was razed with the rest of Anscombe's establishment in

The Regent Harpenden , probably taken during the 1950s. The shop to the right of the entrance is the Regent Bag Shop. (Courtesy of Eric Brandreth.)

the summer of 1983 to make way for the Waitrose supermarket which continues to trade in 2002.

Wednesday 27 November 1935

Austral / Embassy
Luton Road

Having sold the Victoria Theatre, Captain F. A. Webb returned quite soon to the cinema scene in Harpenden by acquiring part of the Rectory garden on the outskirts of the town centre for a modern purpose-built luxury cinema which he called the Austral – short for Australia, his homeland. The cinema's advertising logo included a kangaroo! It had an 870-seat auditorium built on the stadium plan with a raised rear section and lower ceiling than if a proper balcony had been included. The architects were T. H. Johnson and Son of Doncaster. The rather plain but spacious auditorium had a predominantly brown and ivory colour scheme with green carpet and upholstery on the seats. It had a Holophane lighting installation by which 'symphonies' of slowly changing colours could be played on the curtains, proscenium coves and ceiling. The owner's son, Gus Webb, was the first manager and *Cardinal Richelieu* with George Arliss was the first feature shown.

The cinema was far more respectable than the Regent and played new releases, though not as early as St Albans where Captain Webb ran the Chequers. After he died, aged 80, in January 1951, the cinema was acquired by circuit magnate W. Southan Morris and underwent a change of name to Embassy later that year. It was one of the few cinemas that Morris did not sell to Essoldo in 1954 and it was very much his pride and joy and the only cinema he still owned at the time of his death in 1979. It was then run by Southan Morris's daughter, Mrs Sheila Daykin, and his son, Stewart Morris, but it had fallen from favour with the local population who stayed away even though it offered a huge screen and excellent sightlines.

The auditorium of the Austral (later Embassy) Harpenden in 1935.

The car park was shared with the adjacent garage run by Ogglesby's, which acquired the fading cinema in 1983 to ensure that its customers would still have somewhere to park. Ogglesby's took over running the cinema but found that some evenings no one bothered to turn up. The garage declared that mounting losses and a £30,000 estimate for repairs prompted their decision to close the Embassy. 1,700 people signed a petition asking for the cinema to be retained (although, of course, they did not turn up in a sudden rush to buy tickets).

If it had to go, at least the Embassy went out in style. Its final attractions were special ones – *That's Entertainment!* on the final Thursday, *South Pacific* on Friday and Saturday, and for the last day – Sunday 30 October 1983 – *Gone with the Wind*, starting at 6.45pm.

The Embassy Harpenden in October 1983. (Photograph by Eric Meadows. Courtesy of Eric Brandreth.)

By the end of January 1984, the Embassy had also gone with the wind. In June 1984, a new Ogglesby's petrol station and car wash occupied the front of the site with a storage area for new cars at the rear. Ogglesby's continue to trade there in 2002.

HATFIELD

Monday 7 October 1935

Regent / Odeon / Classic / Curzon

46 The Common

A modest 700-seater built to the plans of E. B. Parkinson, the new Regent was the first purpose-built cinema in Hatfield. The Public Hall on London Road had been used from 1913 to 1925 for occasional shows (it had a capacity of around 350) while the

Workhouse was also licensed for the same purpose in 1913. The Public Hall was hired by the management of the Welwyn Garden City Kinema to become the Picture House from Friday 26 June 1925 but this operated on Friday evenings only at first, opening on Mondays as well the following year, and on Mondays, Tuesdays and Thursdays in 1928. In June 1935 it became the Regent and operated full-time for a few months as a prelude to the opening of the new Regent.

In May 1935 a prominent cinema figure, D. J. James, acquired a site on the Barnet By-Pass (by the private road to the De Havilland aerodrome and near the junction with St Albans Road) for a huge 1,803-seat cinema (1,284 stalls and 519 balcony) with ballroom, café, adjacent shops and parking space for 1,000 cars. This was to be designed on similar or identical lines to his Mayfair (later Odeon) at Whalebone Lane, South Dagenham, by architects Kemp and Tasker. Observing the smaller cinema being built in a more central position, Mr James arranged to purchase this as it neared completion and scrapped his own plans.

The new Regent was somewhat economically built with panels tacked to the ceiling rather than plasterwork (as was done at the Odeon Barnet, by a different architect). The wide auditorium had parallel sidewalls with a line of concealing lighting in the cornice extending along the sides of the small balcony with its six straight rows (reached by a staircase from the right-hand side of the compact foyer). The curved ceiling was

The rather plain exterior and auditorium of the Regent Hatfield at opening in 1935. It is very similar in shape to the Studio Elstree, by the same architect for the same original promoter. Note the unusual placement of a round clock in the top of the proscenium. See back cover for a similar view with the curtains parted. (Author's collection, courtesy of T. J. Braybon and John Fernee).

rather low and left little room for the projection beam from the box at the back which could easily be obstructed by an upheld hand. A car park at the rear could hold 200 vehicles.

Within a year or so, D.J. James sold his circuit to General Cinema Finance, the company in which J. Arthur Rank began his interest in film exhibition which soon extended to control of the vast Odeon and Gaumont circuits. By the spring of 1943, GCF cinemas had become part of Odeon, which had acquired a site in Hatfield for a cinema before the war (it was sold in the early 1950s). It was only a matter of time before the Regent was re-named Odeon (from Monday 7 October 1946). The Hatfield theatre generally played films a month or more after St Albans and most bookings were for three days rather than a week as audiences had been siphoned off by the cinemas of St Albans (easily reached by bus) or Welwyn Garden City (favoured by those with cars).

The Odeon became one of forty-seven weaker cinemas disposed of as going concerns by the Rank Organisation to the Classic circuit in December 1967. On Sunday 17 December the cinema took the Classic name but its new owners found it difficult to operate successfully and in February 1969 a twenty-one year lease was granted to the Panton company which took over and re-named it the Curzon from Sunday 16th of that month.

Panton launched the Chequers Bingo and Social Club at the Curzon on Wednesday 16 April 1969 (the company ran Chequers Bingo in St Albans). Films now played five days of the week with bingo on Wednesdays and Thursdays. Bingo was added on Sunday afternoons from July 1969, and soon spread to Fridays and Saturdays, restricting films to Sunday, Monday and

View of the Regent Hatfield's auditorium in 1935 showing the small, distant balcony, the concealed lighting along the top of the side walls and the chunky art deco light fittings in the ceiling. A curtain at the back of the stalls covers the entrance doors.

Tuesday plus a Saturday matinée and extra afternoon shows in school holidays. Apart from Sunday, cinema had been relegated to the worst days of the week and, not surprisingly, it ceased altogether after *The Godfather* played a two-week run on the days available, the last picture show being the film's Saturday matinée-only screening on 2 June 1973. Bingo took over full time. The screen was removed but the closed curtains remained, as did the projectors for many years.

In the 1980s the first consent was obtained to replace the building with business accommodation. The site was sold at auction in September 1991 when Panton was paying £15,000 per annum under a lease extended to 1996 which could, however, be terminated at three months' notice. A local businessman acquired the property and ended the run of Chequers bingo. The building stood disused. New consent was obtained in 1996 for demolition and redevelopment. But, the building re-opened as the New Chequers Bingo Club in 1998. An application for renewal of the 1996 consent was made in the spring of 2001. However, the threat of replacement by small business units, car parking and a landscaped area seems to have receded as, behind a somewhat faded exterior display, the buildings continues as a well-appointed bingo hall in early 2002, its stalls area now filled with tables but its balcony still retaining its rows of cinema seats and its picture house atmosphere.

Wednesday 25 and Friday 27 September 1991

UCI

The Galleria, Comet Way

After the closing of the Curzon, a new cinema was to be included in a town centre redevelopment by the Greyhound Racing Association in 1976 but the potential operator went into liquidation and the GRA were unable to find anyone else interested in fitting out the space for a 280-seat auditorium. Plans for an American-style drive-in cinema on an 18-acre site near Hatfield in 1975 also came to nought. A twin cinema was then envisaged for space above the Tempo store but this became a squash club instead. When the Forum leisure centre was built in the late 1970s, no provision for showing films was originally made but they were tried out, beginning with a week's run of *The Final Countdown* on 1 September 1980, and were subsequently shown on occasion.

The preferred site for an American-style multiplex was one immediately accessible from a motorway so that it could attract audiences from a greater distance. It would be hard to better the location of this £5 million UCI multiplex which opened as part of

the Galleria shopping mall (pronounced Galler-re-a) built directly over the A1 (M) tunnel near junction 23 of the M25. And yet, in this case, it was also very close to the town centre rather than being some distance away.

Britt Ekland was the special guest invited to perform the official opening ceremony on Wednesday 25 September 1991, with the chairman of Hatfield Town Council attending. Regular public performances started two days later with nine major films – *Stepping Out, Jacob's Ladder, Teen Agent, Under Suspicion, True Identity, Life Stinks, Regarding Henry, Terminator 2* and *Robin Hood Prince of Thieves* – in the nine auditoria which seated 172, 235, 263, 167, 183, 183, 260, 378 and 172. Prices of admission were £3.75 for adults (£2.75 before 6pm) and £2.25 for children, students and seniors. In the Cinema Theatre Association *Bulletin* (Jan/Feb 1992), Andy Cremer commented: "It must surely be the only cinema built on top of a motorway! The exterior is unbelievably bland, and is overshadowed by the huge bulk of the shopping mall behind. It can only be assumed that the architect of the cinema drew his inspiration from a chest freezer with a parrot cage on top! However, the foyer is spacious and airy, with cove lighting and the usual array of fast food outlets. The auditorium I visited was very plain and had no screen tabs, but the presentation and comfort were excellent." Parking spaces and fast food establishments were close by.

Visited in January 2002, the Galleria as a whole looked rather frayed, past its best-by date. The multiplex occupies a large, ugly box-like structure raised off the ground on columns, with an escalator to the foyer and emergency exit stairs descending elsewhere. The complex is connected to the main Galleria by a first-floor passage with shops

alongside, passing an open ground-floor car park. The exterior has UCI cinema signs externally on both sides but the titles of the films showing are displayed only through a large window at the front of the foyer by the top of the escalator. Reached by a few further steps, the wide foyer is low-ceilinged with video screens and concealed uplighting set in the upper side walls. The diagonal pattern in the large open floor is crudely interrupted by rectangular access covers to what lies beneath. The cinema was refurbished in 1994 just before the nearby Odeon multiplex opened at Hemel Hempstead and looks as clean and smart as possible. It is a maxim in the cinema business that the three most important factors in building a cinema are "location, location, location" and the UCI has that in spades.

The UCI Hatfield multiplex in 2002. The escalator to the foyer can be seen through the ground floor windows in the view across the car park. Interior view shows the head of the escalator, the box-office at far right, and steps to the foyer in the centre. (Both photographed by Allen Eyles.)

HEMEL HEMPSTEAD

Friday 17 December 1909

Electric Theatre / Aero

Albion Hill

T he Salvation Army's Albion Hall was turned into a 180-seat Electric Theatre that left a few things to be desired. The seating consisted of forms with wooden backs and a licensing report in February 1910 referred to only two exits, one of which passed under staging for apparatus. It recommended that a further exit be provided, besides noting that the central gangway was only 2ft 8ins wide rather than a more desirable 3ft.

Shows were continuous from 6.30 pm to 10.30pm with three changes weekly. "People's popular prices" of threepence and sixpence were charged, rising to sixpence and one shilling on Saturdays. There were reduced prices for children and a special 3pm matinée for them on Saturdays (admission: 1d, 2d and 3d). In 1912 the cinema seems to have added a new stage in a yard at the back. It was still open in 1913 but not licensed for 1916.

An early photograph of the Princess.

Enlarged to seat 300, it re-opened as the Aero in 1920 with films accompanied by the Aero Orchestra. Seats now cost fivepence, eightpence, one shilling, and 1/3d. In 1922 the Aero closed from the end of May to Monday 7 August for alterations. A new, larger Aero was later planned on a different site and this Aero's last show was a three-day run of Tom Mix in *Conquering Blood* ending on Saturday 17 July 1926, three days before its replacement opened. The building has long been demolished and today the site, according to local historian Tony Rogers, "is in the middle of the Marlowes shopping mall around the Tie Rack area."

Monday 23 December 1912

Princess

Marlowes

W . H. Barton of Esher was the architect for this cinema, built in ten weeks on a single floor with a small stage and seating around 600 with two private boxes. Bill Groom, a reader of the local *Gazette*, provided the newspaper's 'Heritage Extra' section dated 16 August 2000 with some memories of the Princess in its early years:

"There was no electricity supply in the town, so they had to generate their own. They had a detached building at the rear where there were two engines to generate the power. The owners were George Allanston and Walter Greey, who had a furniture shop in the High Street and was also an auctioneer. They had two shows every weekday with an added matinée on Saturday…. The prices were – wooden seats in the front 5d, cushion seats below the gangway 8d, above the gangway, 1/- then 1/3d, and two private boxes at 5/- each. Half price for children. The programme was Pathé Gazette with the latest news. Then a short comedy, with Charlie Chaplin, Harold Lloyd, Buster Keaton, Laurel and Hardy and many more, next a serial to be continued next week, this with Pearl White and Warner Oland.

"The man who operated the cinema was Wally Pratt, a big ex-policeman... He would put on a boiler suit, and start one of the engines for charging up and when things were going smoothly, he would go into a cubbyhole, and come out with his commissionaire's uniform on – peak cap, his jacket was covered in gold braid, with gold epaulettes, trousers with red ribbons up the seams and very shiny boots, he was now ready for work. He would go to the forecourt and parade, and kept the youngsters in order until the doors were opened.

"The rest of the staff were Miss Floe Allaston [Allanston?] in the paybox. She was a most imposing sight, her bottle-blonde hair was piled on her head, she was past the first flush of youth but she did her best. She was heavily powdered and painted, long drop earrings down to her shoulders, sleeveless blouse revealed much cleavage, all very attractive. Next we had the three Tavener brothers, Albert, the eldest, he did a lot of dashing about and was the boss. Then Percy, who stood at the entrance and tore the tickets in half, then Sid who went round with the chocolate tray; but in my opinion, the most important was George Motherwell, the pianist... Each evening, as regular as clockwork, he would make his way to work, he called at the Sebright Arms to get his bottles of beer, and then to the cinema. His piano was in the orchestra pit. He eased the top off his bottles and put a couple on the top of the piano. He had to start playing ten minutes before the show started and he had a few minutes [off] in the middle of the first house. George had a limited repertoire but he kept pace with the films. There was a projectionist and a lad, George Miller, who later

The Princess on its final day of operation in 1962. (Photograph by Alan Willmott. Courtesy of Tony Rogers.)

was manager. I do not think a lot of money was made, although Friday and Saturday always seemed to be busy. I once went to a Wednesday afternoon show, there were four of us paying customers. They gave us tickets for the evening show and then closed the place up."

In the summer of 1925, the Princess was acquired by Captain F. A. Webb, who features in the cinema history of Harpenden and St Albans. It stayed on silent films months after its rival, the Aero/Luxor, installed sound. There was a further change of ownership and it closed for alterations on Saturday 13 December 1930, re-opening on Boxing Day with talkies.

Around 1943 it was acquired by SM Super Cinemas, a circuit operated by Southan Morris which already had the town's Luxor. In the late 1940s the second projectionist at the Princess was Les Bowie, who in 1968 won a Hollywood Oscar for the special effects on *Superman*.

Both the Princess and Luxor became part of the Essoldo chain when that took over SM in 1954. The pair were doomed by the New Town shopping centre development plans but the Princess's site was not required as early as that of the Luxor. It had suspended weekday matinées and generally played second fiddle to the Luxor but, once that had gone, it re-opened during afternoons and gave the town's new Odeon a run for its money with aggressive press advertising. The Princess took the weekly ABC circuit release as well as some of the 'National Release' selections, and so it did not starve for strong programmes. However, a compulsory purchase order forced its closure on 24 February 1962 after a three-day run of the Jerry Lewis comedy *The Errand Boy* supported by *Hey, Let's Twist*. It was quickly demolished. Its site is pinpointed by Tony Rogers as having been where trees now

The Luxor in 1949 when postwar lighting restrictions were lifted and cinemas were allowed to switch on their neon. (Courtesy of Dacorum Heritage via Tony Rogers.)

stand to the front and to the left of the Civic Centre.

Boxing Day 1924

Aero / Central Hall Cinema

Orchard Street and Manor Avenue, Apsley

The proprietors of the Aero on Albion Hill leased the Apsley Memorial Hall in the southern part of the town and turned this into a second Aero cinema which sometimes played the same films (the reels were presumably bicycled between the two halls). It was open six days a week. When the lease was dropped in early January 1926, a Mr Stringer operated the property as the Central Hall Cinema from Monday 11 January to Saturday 5 June. The building was used for occasional film shows in later years and still stands as the premises of the First Stop garage.

Tuesday 20 July 1926

Aero / Luxor

Marlowes

The new Aero was built for S. Nicholls of Luton and his partner, R. Coles, to replace their Aero on Albion Hill and to provide a suitable counter attraction to the amusements in Watford which were said to draw a thousand people from Hemel Hempstead each Saturday, even in winter.

The architect was H. R. Finn of St Albans and the Aero took eighteen months to erect. It seated a total of 760: 561 in the stalls, 199 in the balcony. The opening day coincided with a visit by HRH The Prince of Wales to see the town but his itinerary did not include taking in the first night of the new

The Luxor on its last day of operation in August 1960. (Photograph by Alan Willmott. Courtesy of Tony Rogers.)

Aero. Nevertheless, he became part of the evening as film of his visit was processed and rushed from London to be shown around 10pm. After that, the Erich von Stroheim feature *The Merry Widow* was screened. People had to be turned away – in part because not all the seats had been put up in time! The £2,000 pipe organ had not been finished either, but Edgar Smith, organist of the Aeolian Hall, performed as best he could and also demonstrated the new grand piano. Well-known soprano Carrie Tubbs was the star live attraction and she received three encores. In all, the opening show lasted five and a half hours and ended just before midnight when, as the local press put it, "everyone went home utterly tired but unspeakably happy".

Space was available for parking cars and leaving bicycles. Seats could be booked in advance and prices ran from sixpence to

two shillings for the "balcony alcove". The Aero Orchestra performed nightly in the orchestra pit, accompanying the silent films, while variety artists took to the stage between the films. The stage (20ft wide, 16ft deep) had ample wing space and there were three dressing rooms and a large band room under the stage

Silver King was the last silent film shown and the date was Saturday 3 May 1930. Renamed the Luxor (reflecting the interest in the findings at the great pyramids at the place of the same name), the cinema re-opened the following Monday with *The Sky Hawk*, heard on Western Electric sound. A new screen had been installed 7ft further back on the stage, smaller in size so that it could be seen from the front row. Live variety still supported the films as late as 1932. Live shows sometimes replaced films entirely, as when the local Operatic Society moved in on dates as far apart as 1930 and 1954 (the latter, a three-day run of *The Arcadians*).

In October 1936 the Luxor became the first of a new circuit built up by Southan Morris after his acrimonious departure from the position of general manager of the Union circuit. It then had 718 seats and soon styled itself "The Luxurious Luxor". Morris added the Princess to his chain during the war. Eileen George, now living in St Leonards, East Sussex, remembers visiting both the Princess and the Luxor during the Second World War: "The Luxor was the posher of the two cinemas. If we entered the Princess, we would surely catch nits. That did not put us off! The programmes were continuous, so we tried to stay to watch the film twice. Unfortunately, we were often spotted and asked to leave that magical place."

Tony Rogers, who started work at the Luxor cinema in 1948 as rewind boy, recalls: "In 1948 new projection equipment was installed. This was state-of-the-art equipment for the time and consisted of Gaumont Kalee type 21 projectors and the new Westrex sound system. The old Kalee model 12s were transferred to the Princess where they continued to operate with the old battery-operated Western Electric sound system until the Princess was closed in 1962. In the early 1950s one of the projectionists at the Luxor was Alan Bailey who went on to become a very well known sound engineer who recorded Beatles and Monty Python records."

As previously mentioned in connection with the Princess, Essoldo took over Southan Morris's circuit, including his two

Hemel Hempstead cinemas, in 1954. The Luxor was forced to close, not by declining audiences but to make way for town centre redevelopment. A seven-day revival of Cecil B. DeMille's epic *Samson and Delilah* ending on Saturday 27 August 1960 was its parting attraction. Demolition soon followed.

Tony Rogers, who had risen to chief projectionist of the Luxor when it closed, comments: "Many local publications, whenever they mention the Luxor cinema, say it was where the Woolworth store is today. This is incorrect as Woolworth's was open to the public many months before the Luxor closed in 1960. The cinema stood next to Woolworth's and where the Etam ladies' clothes store is today."

Monday 29 August 1960

Odeon

Marlowes (corner of Coombe Street)

There had been interest in building new cinemas in Hemel Hempstead in the 1930s: a 1,351-seat Lyric to plans of F. E. Tasker near the junction of St Albans Road and Marlowes in 1936, and an Embassy (or Rex) with 1,700 seats (architect: Robert Cromie) at Moor End House, by a railway

The Odeon Hemel Hempstead shortly after opening in 1960. The film on the canopy is a Sunday revival. (Photograph by Allen Eyles.)

bridge adjacent to Wood Lane, in 1937. But it was not until 1960 that Hemel Hempstead received a new cinema as part of a short-lived programme by the Rank Organisation to open Odeons in New Towns. The Harlow Odeon came first, Hemel Hempstead was next, and others at Crawley and Stevenage were planned but not built. The site in Hemel Hempstead was between the Princess and Luxor, on the same side of Marlowes as they were.

The new Odeon was designed by Robert Bullivant, one of the partners of Harry Weedon and Partners (Bullivant had designed many pre-war Odeons including the now listed ones at Chester, Leicester, Rhyl and York). There were subsoil problems that halted work in spring 1959 but the foundation stone was laid later that year by Lauren Bacall (who was then starring opposite Kenneth More in the film *North West Frontier* for Odeon's parent company, The Rank Organisation). The Odeon was completed at a building cost of £108,734 15s 2d with architects' fees a further £6,922 0s 10d and quantity surveyor's fees amounting to £3,454 11s 5d. The cinema had a low entrance with a surprisingly small foyer that allowed space for a cramped manager's office to one side. The single-floor auditorium held 1,148 seats with generous spacing between rows – half the seats were on a raked floor and half on 5ft steppings at the back. There was an almost horizontal throw to the huge screen in the 63ft-wide proscenium opening, and ten auditorium effects speakers were placed in the side and rear walls. The Odeon offered a lavish, pleasing environment for seeing films on a huge screen and particularly good sightlines. Initial prices of admission were 2/6d (12½p) and 3/6d. There was a Presto fast food establishment attached to the Odeon, to the right of the entrance, masking the auditorium

The curtains have been opened to show the huge screen in the spacious auditorium of the Odeon Hemel Hempstead in 1960.

block on Marlowes although its side wall was evident down Coombe Street at the corner.

The Odeon was opened by the Mayor with a special screening of the Rank comedy *Doctor in Love* and personal appearances by two of the stars, Leslie Phillips and Virginia Maskell. In effect, it replaced the town's Luxor, also in Marlowes, which was closed the preceding Saturday, but it still had to share the new releases with the Princess for its first eighteen months of operation. There was some disappointment when films played the Odeons at Watford and St Albans weeks and even months before Hemel Hempstead and this has been blamed on the poor attendances that soon followed. In 1973 Rank wanted to switch over to bingo on Thursdays, Fridays and Saturdays – normally the busiest days of the week for cinema-going, apart from Sunday. The Borough Council suggested Mondays, Tuesdays and Wednesdays and after much negotiation consent was finally given for bingo on Wednesdays, Thursdays and Fridays with films continuing on the other four days of the week. The Odeon closed temporarily after Saturday 23 March 1974 for adjustments to be made to accommodate bingo. The Top Rank Club opened on Wednesday 27 March with star appearances by Pete Murray, Tony Blackburn and Ed Stewart on the first three nights. Films resumed on Saturday 30 March with a one-day presentation of two Elvis Presley documentaries, then the following day Clint Eastwood's *Magnum Force* inaugurated the four-day film runs. In all, 785 cinema seats were retained, along with the huge screen. This limited playing time further hindered the Odeon in obtaining current films and confused filmgoers, but the popularity of bingo supported the cinema side. At a few other Odeons where the Rank Organisation split the week between films and bingo, the eventual result was full-time bingo or closure, but the Hemel Hempstead Odeon continued its awkward marriage of rival entertainments, by 1988 ceding the best day of the week, Saturday, to bingo. By this time, rows of fruit machines also filled the foyer. Even though Dolby stereo sound was fitted, it is obvious that bingo had the upper hand as films were not only cut back to three days a week but confined to

Sunday and the two worst days for cinema-going – Monday and Tuesday. Then a modern Odeon multiplex cinema was included in the plans for the new Leisure World at Jarman Park, and it was obvious that films would cease at the town centre site when it opened.

In 1994 an application was granted for bingo on seven days a week, months before the multiplex was ready, prompting a petition supported by Leslie Phillips, who had helped to open the cinema in 1960, that films should continue to be shown at least until the replacement opened. This, in fact, is what happened and films ceased at the Odeon on 22 August 1995, only three days before the opening of its successor.

Being aimed at a young clientèle, Jarman Park did not include a bingo club, and the old Odeon was used for full-time bingo as part of the Jasmine chain. This could not have been a success as the building has since been converted into a public house by the Wetherspoon chain. The pub was launched under the name of The Full House on 21 July 1998. While Wetherspoon's have often preserved much of the character of old cinemas, even when the buildings have been unlisted (as at Holloway Road, north London, and at Walsall), here virtually every trace of the old foyer and auditorium was eliminated. The pub uses little more than the rear half of the wide auditorium and has a fake proscenium arch, much more elaborate than the one the Odeon had, erected across the new end wall enclosing a panoramic view of an Armageddon-like scene painted on part of the old cinema screen. Part of the plain auditorium ceiling can be seen with its embedded house lights (no longer in use) and some plain original grille work is visible across the old back wall. Otherwise, an entirely new decorative scheme has been imposed (and was due to be modified in mid-2002 during a short period of closure). The two film projectors remain in the old projection room, now used as a store room. The former restaurant on the corner of the site next to the entrance has been demolished to create an outdoor drinking area enclosed by a low wall and shrubs.

Friday 25 August 1995

Odeon

Leisure World, Jarman Park

The entrance to the Odeon at one end of Hemel Hempstead's Leisure World, seen past litter-strewn waste ground. (Photograph by Allen Eyles.)

The new eight-screen Odeon was part of the Rank Organisation's £22 million edge-of-town multi-leisure development which created the largest leisure centre of its kind in Europe. The site was originally known as Jarman Fields and was indeed occupied by fields but has now become Jarman Park. The development offered a variety of amusements beside the cinemas, including the Hotshots and Jumpin' Jaks night clubs, the Aqua Splash water adventure park, the Silver Blades ice skating rink and ten-pin bowling. Burger King and Pizza Hut outlets plus various bars were also featured. This was Rank's sixth multi-leisure park in the United Kingdom and it was calculated that the location near the M1, the M25 and the A41 meant that 1.6 million people could drive there within forty minutes. The architects for the whole scheme were the London practice of S & P.

The new multiplex not only brought about the end of part-week films at the town centre Odeon but also led, less justifiably, to the shutting of the three-screen Odeon at St Albans, several miles to the east.

Within Leisure World, the Odeon is at the left end of the site with the corner being given over to Pizza Hut. There is a general entrance to the leisure centre to the right of Pizza Hut and the Odeon's box-office is inside on the left with a long foyer directly behind, reached by steps or a ramp. There are eight cinemas seating 120, 170, 170, 276, 210, 401, 152 and 152. Originally six screens were planned but the space was reconfigured to provide two more. Five of the cinemas have entrances down the left of the long inner foyer with others at the far end and to

The foyer to the Odeon multiplex at Hemel Hempstead with the auditoria reached by the steps in the background. (Photograph by Allen Eyles.)

the right. The entrance hall also provides direct access to Jumpin' Jaks on the right and leads to the other attractions.

There is a car park to the left of the building from which one is made only too aware of the complex's corrugated side wall, painted in four horizontal bands of sickly shades from ochre through two shades of yellow to a cream base. With its bleak wasteland approach, Jarman Park is a particularly unattractive structure externally. At least it is well away from the town centre.

HERTFORD

Monday 14 November 1910

People's Electric Theatre

2a Maidenhead Street
(corner with Bull Plain)

This was a conversion of part of the premises of Messrs J. J. Rayment and Son into a cinema seating 160 persons (it was a month later said to accommodate 260 persons but this may take into account standing room). The proprietor was C. E. Sheppard while E. S. Peeke was the operator (i.e. projectionist) and electrician.

We find Mr Sheppard stating in an advertisement which appeared on 25 October 1913: " … in view of the rumours that the [Theatre] is shortly to be closed [he] wishes to state that he has the hall on a lease for a number of years and the cinema will continue as usual." However, it closed around September 1914 when Mr Sheppard acquired the rival Premier cinema.

The premises were for many years a branch of Boots but by 1985 they were occupied by F. Hinds, jewellers, who continue in business there in 2002.

Saturday 24 December 1910

Premier / Popular Picture Playhouse / Premier Theatre Of Varieties / Regent

1 Market Street

The Premier was purpose-built for Harry R. D. Hooper on part of the site of the

White Hart Hotel and had approximately 220 seats. A small orchestra accompanied the silent films and after C.E. Sheppard became proprietor and manager in late 1914 live variety acts were included in the programmes. (During this First World War period, the Corn Exchange seems to have been a rival, showing occasional films as the Kinetic Picture Palace with a capacity of 500.)

Tom E. Davies took over from Sheppard in 1920, re-opening the cinema as the Popular Picture Playhouse on Monday 20 December but films seem to have stopped after Saturday 24 September 1921. By the mid-1920s it was leased to C. and H. Bailey and run as the Premier Theatre of Varieties, dropping films in favour of live shows usually featuring seven performers. It remained a live theatre until early April 1929 when it closed "temporarily" but did not re-open in September as promised.

Films returned after sound was installed and it became the 200-seat Regent cinema on Monday 26 September 1932 under the control of J. Howard, succeeded later by J. H. Gotch and by the E. Owen Cooper Theatres circuit. Despite its minute size, it managed to compete with the Castle and County cinemas not only because of its very central location but because it offered the only three penny seats in town (the other two started at sixpence).

Hertfordshire resident Ronald Wright recalls: "In the early 1930s my mother was a cleaner at the Regent cinema. On Saturday mornings I would go to work with her and while she did the cleaning I would search under all the seating for sweets and coins which the audience (I hoped) had dropped the night before. Sometimes, too, much to the irritation of my mother, the young projectionist would plunge the place into darkness suddenly in order to try a bit of the

The Premier Hertford, circa 1911.

following week's movie which had just been received. I loved this, of course. My mother got free tickets for the Regent, and so I used to go there at least twice a week."

The Regent closed in May 1943 but the premises survived, the auditorium area being used in 1985 by the engineering firm of Wharton and Wilcox and the front section forming the premises of Jangles, the hairdressers. In 2002 the hairdressers in residence style themselves Fringe Benefits.

Thursday 13 August 1914

Castle

7 The Wash

The Castle Cinema was a further business venture by William Skipp who had opened the Ware Picture Hall in 1911. The builders were John Ray Ltd who later built the County and five other cinemas in Hertfordshire. There was said to be an exceptionally deep slope to the floor affording a clear view of the screen and it was reported to have 1,000 seats when it opened. Prices were then 3d, 6d, 1/- and 2/- so that the most expensive seats cost eight

The Castle Hertford, circa 1914. (Courtesy of Cyril Heath.)

times as much as the cheapest (where you sat was an indication of economic and social status). Free storage was offered to patrons who arrived by bicycle. An orchestra accompanied the films in the silent days. The Castle remained in the Skipp family (although it was run, along with the Popular Picture Playhouse, by Tom E. Davies in the early 1920s) until in June 1933 it was taken over by the Hitchin syndicate which opened the new County cinema in the following month. Both cinemas were

The Castle Hertford in the 1950s. (The Cinema Museum.)

then sold to the Shipman & King circuit in April 1938.

Although the County showed the most important films, there were still plenty of new releases to keep the Castle going, usually with a mid-week change of programme. S & K closed the Castle on 3 June 1939 for thorough modernisation to plans of Howis and Belcham. It re-opened on Monday 9 October with a modern, plain frontage and new foyer as well as a new central heating plant. The seating capacity became around 600.

The Castle's progress was interrupted by a German flying bomb which exploded on the Sunday morning of 2 July 1944 causing considerable damage not only to the Castle but to the Mill next door and the ARP headquarters on the other side of the River Lea. The Castle was eventually patched up and re-opened on Monday 2 September 1946 with a six-day run of *I See a Dark Stranger*, including daily matinées. By the mid-1950s the Castle had a matinée on Saturday only and opened other days around 4.30pm while the more favoured County was functioning from 2pm daily. Declining attendances meant insufficient business for two cinemas in Hertford and the Castle closed down on Saturday 28 November 1959 after a three-day run of a minor drama, *The City Jungle*, starring Paul Newman.

It stood boarded-up and derelict for many years until it was demolished and the site used as a temporary car park. The impressive new civic centre, Castle Hall, was then built on the space and besides such events as wrestling, concerts, amateur theatricals, stamp fairs and antique shows, there have been screenings of films on certain days each month by a film society.

Monday 10 July 1933

County

Ware Road

Hertford's most impressive cinema was built on the edge of the town centre where sufficient space for a large building and car park was more readily available. It was erected by the same group of people who had promoted the Hermitage at Hitchin the previous year although a separate company was formed. It again featured Edgar Simmons (the architect and chairman), John Ray (the builder), L. E. Agar (managing director) and J. G. Wainwright (head of a separate circuit of cinemas).

The Hertford County was very similar in style to the Hitchin cinema as well as to the Barnet Odeon and Reading Granby that

The lofty auditorium of the County Hertford in October 1982 seen under the stark cleaners' lights. Note the original light fitting on the wall at left. (Adapted from a colour transparency by Allen Eyles.)

Simmons designed later. The colonnade in the centre of the frontage above the entrance doors displayed the elongated arches with a distinctive, rather Oriental shape that Simmons used in all these cinemas but there are many other recurring external details. However, the County did have the distinctive touch of two massive, free-standing boxes set in the foot of the entrance steps next to the pavement, carrying display cases advertising the current programme. The auditorium was markedly similar in style to other cinemas by Simmons – including the intricate pattern in the ceiling.

The County opened with a double bill of Marlene Dietrich in *Blonde Venus* and George Raft in *Undercover Man*. It seated 580 in the stalls and 578 in the balcony – an unusual near-equal distribution of the seats. There was a 20 foot deep stage and eight dressing rooms, and sometimes films made way for local dramatic and operatic productions or a Christmas pantomime on tour from London (*Cinderella* and *Aladdin* are ones that are still remembered). There was a café for many years, located upstairs in the

The County Hertford, circa 1964. (See also front cover.)

circle lounge with its open-air balcony behind the tall arches.

The S & K circuit took over the County (along with the Castle) from its first owners in April 1938 and it continued to be a successful cinema for many years, playing the most important pictures and leaving the rest for the Castle. It retained weekday matinées long after they were discontinued at the Castle and out-survived the older cinema by twenty-two years.

In 1972 plans were drawn up to split the building for a 500-seat cinema in the circle area and a 450-seat bingo club to be operated by the Star Group downstairs. In 1974 Mecca was interested in purchasing it and spending £100,000 on converting the entire building to bingo but neither change took place. Some slight modernisation was carried out in later years. A new vertical sign appeared in the centre replacing the name on the wings, an illuminated readagraph above the entrance doors gave the current programme details and the two advertising units by the pavement were removed. The foyer was panelled in white with a modern paybox and had all the appeal of a hospital reception area but the auditorium itself remained barely altered. It just became dowdier and dowdier until in its last years the management brought up the house lights as little as possible to hide its drab and dirty appearance. It was no longer an inviting place to spend an evening but there was no willingness on the part of EMI (which had taken over the S & K circuit) to subdivide it into two or three cinemas. Despite an 800-signature protest petition, the County closed on Saturday 16 October 1982 after a week's run of the horror film *The Entity*. It was soon demolished and in 2002 the offices of Graham House and the entrance to Yeomans Court stand in the cinema's place.

Since then Hertford has been a town in search of a cinema. A petition with 700 signatures persuaded the Council to invite cinema schemes. In 1996 East Hertfordshire District Council tried to interest a developer in providing leisure facilities on a site it owned adjacent to the town centre. An advertisement in trade paper *Leisureweek* (31 May) declared: "The Council believes the site, located near to a bus station, railway station and car park and extends to some 1½ acres, is suitable for its preferred form of development, a 3/4 screen cinema, possibly with a medium sized Ten Pin Bowl operation…. In seeking expressions of interest from commercial developers/operators the Council is responding to the shortfall in entertainment facilities revealed in Mori polling and expressed by the citizens of Hertford and its neighbouring town, Ware." As Hertford still has no cinema in 2002, it is perhaps a pity the Council did not make some effort to save the County, especially as it had facilities for live show use.

Plans have been put forward. One in 1997 for the former Addis site seems to have failed for lack of permission and in April 1998 a London-based company, Metrodome, presented plans for a riverside scheme including small cinemas seating 650 in total, a pub-restaurant and 14-lane bowling alley but these were reported to have fallen through by the end of the year. In December 1999 there was a proposal for a four-screen cinema (the largest auditorium seating 300) above a new Lidl supermarket to be built in Mill Road. The cinema was to cost £1.5m and be open by the end of 2000, operated by Film Network, but Lidl announced that the deal had collapsed because of the cost of outfitting the cinemas.

HITCHIN

Late March 1911

Picturedrome (Blake's Theatre)

Ickleford Road

Having opened a Picturedrome in Bedford, photographic businessmen Jim and Archie Blake chose Hitchin for a second purpose-built cinema. Plans were submitted on 30 January 1911 and the building was completed and inspected on 21 March of that year. Shows combining films with live variety were accompanied by a small orchestra. There was seating for 400 on a single floor. An early attraction was a film made by the Blake brothers of local celebrations for the Coronation of King George V on Thursday 22 June – this was shown the following week.

The Picturedrome's success encouraged others to set about building the Playhouse. The Blakes responded by improving the Picturedrome, adding a gallery to accommodate a further 187 patrons and putting on a new tall front elevation. A new projection box was located under the balcony behind the paybox. The architect for the alterations was E. H. C. Inskip.

While the Picturedrome was temporarily

The Picturedrome Hitchin, with its proprietors' names prominently featured, decorated for the Coronation, June 1911. (Hitchin Museum.)

The Picturedrome Hitchin at right, circa 1916, with a new, taller frontage after a balcony was added. (Hitchin Museum.)

closed, the Blakes took over the New Town Hall in Brand Street for showing pictures from Monday 7 July 1913 to Saturday 4 October – the day the Playhouse opened. The "New Picturedrome" re-opened the following Monday, claiming to be the most central, the best ventilated, and (with ten exits) the safest cinema in town. (The Playhouse was in fact much better positioned.)

The Picturedrome's name was soon accompanied by the slogan "With the Show That's Worth Paying To See". Live entertainment came to be particularly emphasised, from performers like the celebrated Marie Lloyd to boxing matches to amateur talent contests to circus shows including trapeze artists and elephants. By 1921 it had been re-named Blake's Theatre, although films were still shown. The opening of the Hermitage seems to have forced it to go fully live as a variety hall, operated by J. Williams, but in January 1935, after a pantomime and some variety shows, it was taken over, along with the Regal (ex-Playhouse), by the owners of the Hermitage and appears to have been closed.

It re-opened as the Picturedrome on Monday 26 October 1936, with variety acts supporting films at the evening shows and with a policy of catering for children (which lasted only a couple of months). In January 1937 the Picturedrome was given new seating and in February new heating apparatus to prepare it for replacing the Regal (ex-Playhouse) which was closed the following month.

The Picturedrome became redundant with the opening in 1939 of the new Regal nearby in Bancroft. It had turned into the town's 'fleapit' and it closed "for the summer months" on 30 March 1940 after a three-day run of *Bridal Suite* with Annabella and *Jump for Glory* with Douglas Fairbanks Jr. It never re-opened and became a storage depot for the rest of the war. Until late 1963, it appears to have remained derelict, then conversion to industrial use took place and the frontage was completely modernised. In 1984 the premises were used by Kontoor Abrasives and Amwell Electronics Systems, and from October of that year the whole top floor became a health and fitness centre called Active Ingredient.

The Blakes are not forgotten. Since 1973 this spot has been known as Blake's Corner and the name appears on the Post Office next door to the former Picturedrome.

Saturday 4 October 1913

Playhouse / Regal

Market Place

Built for the Hitchin Amusement Company (a local group totalling some 100 shareholders), the Playhouse had a narrow entrance next to the Corn Exchange on the busy Market Square. Patrons passed down a corridor 70ft long by 10ft wide to reach an octagonal-shaped foyer beyond which was the auditorium, seating 750 in stalls and balcony with a private box seating five on each side towards the back. The architect for the Playhouse was Ewen S. Barr. The auditorium seems to have been lavishly decorated with an elaborate painting in the centre of the ceiling and decorated panels on each side wall below seven small circular windows with tinted glass that could be opened. Seventeen gas radiators provided heat. The projection box was placed over the balcony and there was a long 100ft throw to the screen.

The Playhouse was a serious rival to the smaller Picturedrome and also accompanied films with variety acts, but the influx of troops to Bearton camp after the start of World War I ensured prosperity for both halls for a while. In the 1920s the Blake family took over the Playhouse, then in the mid-1930s it came under the same control as the new Hermitage. Early in 1935 it was re-named the Regal and in October it had the latest B.T.H. sound apparatus installed. It then closed on 1 March 1937, supposedly for alterations, while its programmes were transferred to its old rival, the newly improved Picturedrome. It never re-opened and its frontage was absorbed until 1978 by a new branch of Burton's the tailors. In 1985, the newsagents Lavells occupied the area in Market Place.

The Hermitage Hitchin with its later neon sign and the arches that were a trademark feature of cinemas designed by Edgar Simmons. (Courtesy of Ray Price, a former manager.)

Monday 29 February 1932

Hermitage

Hermitage Road

For a little over thirty years, the Hermitage cinema was highly conspicuous with its wide frontage on Hermitage Road. It was designed by Edgar Simmons, who was chairman of the owning company,

and built by John Ray, who was a director. Other directors were L. E. Agar and S. Woods Hill while the Wainwright cinema circuit was financially involved and contributed the operating and film booking expertise. The auditorium's length ran parallel to the road where the side wall of the auditorium was attractively handled with diaper patterns on the brickwork and a cornice with dentils. There were matching corners where Simmons introduced the tall, distinctive arches that were his trademark in cinema design, seen also at the County Hertford and

(top) The Hermitage Hitchin in the summer of 1932. (Courtesy of John Ray via John Squires.)

(left)The auditorium of the Hermitage Hitchin, circa 1932.

Odeon Barnet as well as at the Granby in Reading (where again the columns were on a corner).

The Hermitage seated 1,386: 754 in the stalls and 632 in the large balcony. The tall, ponderously designed auditorium with its central laylight was again very like the later County at Hertford and had many similarities of design with Simmons' other cinemas. There was generous foyer space, a first floor café, and an extensive queueing area inside the building off each side of the stalls (as at the Odeon Barnet), which meant that 750 patrons could wait (half of them seated) for places to become available. In addition, the Hermitage contained a full-size stage, orchestra pit and a dozen dressing rooms, but it lacked an organ and a car park.

With its excellent position and facilities, the Hermitage enjoyed many successful years. The stage was often used for live events – Christmas pantomimes, variety shows, and for local productions by the Hitchin Thespians – but the installation of a CinemaScope screen in the mid-1950s required a large permanent frame on the stage which prevented further theatrical use.

By the early 1960s the Hermitage was still doing well, taking the best films, while the Regal, under the same control, played mostly weaker product or second runs of the hits at the Hermitage. The directors finally decided at a meeting on 19 September 1963 to close the Hermitage on Saturday 28 September and put the valuable site up for sale, expecting that patrons would flock to the Regal instead. The final attraction at the Hermitage was the Peter Sellers comedy *Heavens Above*. The cinema was demolished and replaced by a new Post Office which itself has since closed.

Monday 20 November 1939

Regal

Bancroft

The owners of the Hermitage had obtained the site for a new cinema in Bancroft as far back as 1935 and Edgar Simmons completed his design by mid-October with an announcement that building would start shortly. Simmons provided a façade in Tudor style "to conform, as far as possible, with the ancient character of the Royal Manor town of Hitchin". However, construction did not start until May 1939, probably when John Ray and L. E. Agar of the Hermitage got whiff of a rival scheme.

Two months later, the Berney and Marks group announced its intention to build a cinema between Queen Street and St Andrew's Place (in the area enclosed by Hollow Lane and Lyles Row), for which plans had been drawn up by the leading specialist practice of Andrew Mather. The brisk start of the Bancroft scheme and the outbreak of war in September put an end to this proposal.

By 1939 a Tudor frontage would have seemed very old-fashioned. Taking the Regal name which had been adopted by the Playhouse between 1935 and 1937, the cinema was built to an ultra-modern design by F. E. Bromige (who had seen through Simmons' plans for the Dominion East Barnet after his death) and the frontage, skilfully angled towards the town centre, had large areas of glazing with some of the curved panes and horizontal bars that were a regular feature of Bromige's work and are most conspicuous at his listed cinema at Rayners Lane, Harrow.

Seating 1,055 (approximately 700 in the stalls, 350 in the balcony), the Regal opened with the adventure spectacular *Gunga Din*, plus shorts. In the boom years there were enough popular films to support both the Hermitage and Regal but as attendances declined the best attractions were channelled into the larger, better-sited Hermitage. The Regal was even closed each summer for staff holidays. It did have a large free car park at the rear, entered from Bancroft with an exit onto Fishponds Road, but it was some distance from the town centre.

No auditorium shots have been located for use in this book, which is most regrettable as F. E. Bromige was one of the most adventurous architects of the 1930s with many quite dazzling and unorthodox interiors. He seems to have been on form here, to

The Regal Hitchin in 1979. (Courtesy of Tony Moss.)

judge by these reminiscences contributed by Steve Baker:

"This cinema was particularly kind to patrons queuing because a covered passage adjoined the western flank of the building which could take virtually the whole audience and keep them dry whilst waiting to buy tickets. After climbing the four steps and entering the doors the box office was (latterly) to the left along with the sweet counter.

"The stalls were reached by proceeding up two more steps to an inner foyer, which was offset at a very slight angle to that of the outer (I could never understand why, as the building was rectangular and not a difficult site). The circle stairs were on the far right of the foyer. The circle lounge was enormous and housed several deco settees. The large

Crittal windows were swathed with massive curtains flooded from outside by two powerful lamps.

"A very dark passage and five more steps brought the patron to the middle of the medium-sized circle, the front of which was a shallow curve. The ceiling and walls were orange and there was a striking wavelike-effect mural from the rear of the circle to the front of the stalls ending just short of the ante-proscenium. This was blue and green. There was a stunning curved ceiling down to the proscenium. The tabs were off-white, colour receptive and very slow in opening.

"This cinema, though rectangular rather than 'coffin shaped', was compensated in style by its ceiling design and wall murals which took the patron's eye to the screen. With the warm orange colour and stage lighting, the ambience was superb.

"Unfortunately in 1973, the Regal suffered an arson attack whilst open to the public, causing some to jump from the window onto the canopy below to be rescued. Part of the ceiling sagged and the projectionist, Mr Penny, was the last person to know until his line of vision was obliterated. The cinema was restored in a week or so but never regained popularity and came to a dismal end. Whilst the Regal had no restaurant or tea lounge, it was a most luxurious hall and would today, I am sure, be listed."

The Regal became notorious for its lack of heat – there were no radiators in the auditorium and the only warm air came from its plenum system. It needed the body heat of large audiences to raise the temperature to a satisfactory level and these were no longer in evidence. Seating was uncomfortable and the Regal worsened its image by specialising in sex films even when it was the only cinema in town. It closed on Saturday 23 December 1977 with a typical example – *The Secrets of a Super Stud* – rather than offering more festive fare. Bingo seemed likely but an operating licence was refused in May 1978.

The Regal looked set for a useful new phase of life when it was converted into a recording studio and concert hall that opened in July 1980. Most of the auditorium was retained to provide a 500-seat venue for live music with a large stage in place of the screen. Concerts by top groups like Spandau Ballet, the Thompson Twins, UB40 and John Foxx followed, as well as discos, but it eventually folded and conversion to a snooker hall became a possibility.

However, in the middle of 1985, the Regal stood derelict, waiting to be demolished. As a rare and accomplished example of 1930s architecture in Hitchin, the building even then seemed worth saving to many people. At least three applications were made to have it listed by the Department of the Environment, which would have blocked its demolition, but the DoE found its exterior to be of insufficient architectural or historical value and asked for photographs of its interior. Whether any photographs were forwarded to support the case for listing is not known but, in any case, the Regal had been demolished by spring 1986 and replaced by an office complex called Regal House.

Talk of a three-screen cinema in a new shopping complex in 1990 came to nothing and Hitchin lacks any cinema facility.

HODDESDON

Saturday 15 March 1913

Cinema

Burford Street

It was a race to open a purpose-built cinema in Hoddesdon. The proprietors of the Ware Picture Hall spent months looking for a site and finally in January 1913 announced that they had found one for a 500 – 600-seat cinema. Plans were drawn up for a site 80ft deep by 35ft wide in Duke Street, opposite North Road and the Institute on the corner. However a company headed by A. J. Hatrick beat them to it by opening the Cinema in Burford Street near the river and the Duke Street scheme was dropped.

The Cinema was a quarter of a mile from the town centre down a side road between houses. Local historian E. W. Paddick remembered its early years in a newspaper article. "The films in those days looked as though they'd been photographed in a heavy downpour! The projector was worked by hand and the film was liable to break every few minutes. To while away the time it took to mend it, an elderly man who sincerely believed he could play the violin stood in front and tried to quieten the stamping and catcalls. Sometimes the projector beam couldn't pierce the fug of smoke, as cigarettes were then five for 1½d." Projection was originally from behind the screen across an enclosed dark space (the "focussing room") and had the advantage of removing the audience from immediate danger in the case of fire (which was always a risk with inflammable film and primitive equipment). The building also functioned as a signing-on station during World War I.

In the mid-1920s the Cinema was acquired by the S & K circuit, its first picture house in Hertfordshire. It was closed in early 1930 when S & K opened the larger Pavilion in the town centre.

In the autumn of 1949 the Cinema building was given a new front and converted into the headquarters of the Haileybury Boys Club under the name of the Robert Gilling Hall. The floor was levelled, the old rear projection area became the kitchen and the place looked like any other hall but inside the entrance doors in a 1985 inspection was a paybox window possibly a relic of its cinema days. It continues as the Robert Gilling Hall in 2002.

Monday 3 February 1930

Pavilion

136 High Street

Part of Christie's brewery was saved from demolition to be converted into the Pavilion cinema for the S & K circuit by their architects Howis and Belcham. A narrow entrance was provided from the High Street to the rear of the single-floor auditorium which extended to the left with the screen at right angles to the frontage. A car park was provided alongside the end of the auditorium, off Brewery Road. The opening attraction was the "100% talking, singing, dancing" *Broadway Melody*.

This was a plain, box-like cinema with parallel side walls and a projection room stuck over the rear cross-walk and supported by two pillars. There were 838 seats. Artistic figures decorated panels on the side walls. The ceiling was a simple, shallow curved arch with decorative bands. The cinema had four dressing rooms and facilities for storing scenery so that limited stage shows could be presented. It also had an organ chamber but it was not until 4 September 1933 that Jack Courtnay introduced the newly-installed three-manual six-rank Christie with lift and illuminated console to the Pavilion audience. The organ was also used at religious services that at one time were held on Sundays before the film shows.

In 1938 S & K had Howis and Belcham draw up plans to enlarge the stalls and add a balcony, raising the seating capacity to 1,500 but the scheme was never implemented.

Business began to falter in the 1960s and a bingo licence was obtained in 1971, leading to closure of the Pavilion as a picture house on Saturday 5 February 1972 after a week's run of *The Adventurers*. The organ was then removed. In early March 1972 it became the Star Bingo and Social Club and in 1985 it was run by Zetter's. It then became a Gala club and finally a Cascade club which closed suddenly in September 1997. By this time, the frontage had been reduced in height and was very plain. Its windows were blocked in and the building was demolished a few months later.

By 2002 the entrance area had been replaced by a modern building, occupied by Tollgate Brokers and estate agents Anthony Davies, which joined up with the buildings on either side. At the back there is access to the flats of Brookridge Court, built above the two businesses. A short section of old cinema side wall survives on one side but the auditorium is now occupied by a car park.

Films were subsequently seen in Hoddesdon at the part-time Broxbourne Cinema, established at the Civic Hall in the High Street, and are still part of the schedule in 2002.

The Hoddesdon Pavilion in early 1952. (Courtesy of Lowewood House Museum, Hoddesdon.)

The Hoddesdon Pavilion in 1973, without its ornate canopy.

The Palace Letchworth with its original frontage.

LETCHWORTH

Monday 6 December 1909

Palace

Eastcheap

F ilm pioneer Arthur Melbourne-Cooper followed up the success of his Alpha cinema in St Albans by promoting the Palace at Letchworth. His architects were Barry Parker and Raymond Unwin. The builders were Bennett Bros. The unassuming frontage incorporated two shops and the auditorium seated 750 on a sloping floor (there were also eight boxes at the rear, seating up to five and costing 5/-). It is said to have been the first building in the town centre to have an electricity supply. There were plush 'tip-up' seats at 4d and 6d and plainer seats at 2d. Seats could be booked in advance. Bicycles were stored free. Programmes changed twice weekly. Melbourne-Cooper bowed out in February 1911 and J. F. Bentley took over.

The Palace closed on 6 June 1924 for reconstruction to plans by local architect Edgar Simmons, who became a cinema specialist in the 1930s. An entirely new frontage was built with a large arch, a balcony was added and the roof raised. The boxes remained at the rear of the stalls until 1930 but essentially the Palace had been re-built. There were now around 1,000 seats. It re-opened on Monday 15 September 1924 with a three-day run of the Douglas MacLean comedy *Going Up.*

Betty Jenkins of Hitchin recalls that her father gained the position of musical director at the new Palace. He had previously played as a violinist in Hitchin, first at the Blake's cinema and then, better paid, at the Playhouse. The Palace offered £4 per week, much more than he had been receiving. He continued to play the violin and led six or seven other musicians, including other violinists and cellists. The films were usually delivered with suggestions for an appropriate musical accompaniment and Betty remembers that a harmonium was also used when the silent version of *Ben-Hur* was screened. The musicians also supported the live acts or music hall interludes that were part of the show. Unfortunately, the arrival of talking pictures made them all redundant and Betty's father was one of many who were forced to take up a different profession.

After the opening of the Broadway by the Palace's owners, the older property took a back seat to the almost adjacent newcomer, but there was still enough demand for two cinemas for the next twenty years or so. In 1961 the Palace tried adding live wrestling and this became a monthly event on Wednesdays in 1963. The screen is remembered as having become discoloured in its later years, making black-and-white films look as though they were sepia-tinted. The building itself began to show its age when the licensing authorities demanded improvements to the side exits and the wiring. The balcony exits were attended to in 1975 and early in 1976 the stalls were closed for work downstairs that was never carried out. From December 1976, the Palace lacked a safety certificate for its electrical installations and a year later it was refused a renewal of its cinematograph licence for 1978 until the repairs and rewiring were done. The Palace was still making an operating profit as it hung on to the very last moment, closing on Saturday 31 December 1977 "until further notice", but never re-opened. Indeed, there evidently had been an intention to put the defects right as films had been booked until the end of January. The final programme was the Marty Feldman comedy *The Last Remake of Beau Geste* supported by *The November Plan.*

The end of the Palace caused a major stir. Conservationists, including the Garden City Society, called for the preservation of this "historic" auditorium even though nothing was left of its appearance in 1909. Nevertheless, it could have been adapted to other uses (there was room at the rear to build stage facilities for theatrical use) and *Private Eye* (no. 504, 10 April 1981) scathingly attacked the local authority for converting an old school into a theatre and arts centre when the Palace stood empty. The adjacent disused Fire Station, dating from 1911, was another piece of old Letchworth that many were unhappy to lose. Plans were submitted for shops and offices but the developer then discovered there was no demand for offices. Time and again the wrecker's ball seemed poised to strike and in August/September 1985 the Palace and the old Fire Station finally succumbed to the demolition gang. The Palace was replaced by a £stretcher store with a Blockbuster video store bridging the gap to the Broadway.

The Palace Letchworth, circa 1969.

Monday 4 August 1924

Rendezvous Cinema
Norton Way South

The Rendezvous Cinema was established in the concert hall part of the United Services Club which had been created out of two large Army dining huts brought in sections from Hindhead and re-erected with the help of architect Barry Parker who donated his services. Plays were produced there by Claude Sykes from 1922. The concert hall had a capacity for 800 on a flat floor. There was also a billiard room, reading and cards room, and a kitchen. Films began on the August Bank Holiday Monday in 1924 with Thomas Meighan in *The Ne'er Do Well*, and normally ran three days from Mondays and Thursdays with a small orchestral accompaniment. The immediate popularity of the film shows prompted the London management to raise the floor and fix new seating by Monday 15 September although the whistling and shouting of a gang of lads at the Saturday evening show on 6 September resulted in a ban on under 14s anywhere but in the cheapest 4d seats and the threat of seats at that price being withdrawn.

The Rendezvous promoted itself as "Not the biggest – but the best". Its best seems not to have been good enough. The last advertised show ran from Thursday 31 March 1927 for three days – Estelle Taylor in *Passion's Pathway* – and it is thought to have closed on Saturday 2 April. The Club was demolished in the early 1930s and the site had been taken up by a bowling club for the over-sixties in the mid-1980s.

Wednesday 26 August 1936

Broadway

Gernon Road and Eastcheap

The Broadway was designed by Robert Bennett of Bennett and Bidwell, local architects responsible for much Garden City housing. The promoters ran the Palace and now in this 1,420-seat cinema had a large, more modern cinema as well. (There were 791 seats in the stalls, 629 in the circle.) The brick exterior was unavoidably conspicuous on a prominent corner site but it was tastefully handled. The corner entrance led to an octagonal foyer 12ft high with a central column which carried upward lighting supplemented by light from wall brackets on supporting pillars around the perimeter.

The Broadway Letchworth in 1936.

The auditorium of the Broadway Letchworth in 1936.

There was a cloakroom and a kiosk for purchasing chocolates and cigarettes. On the floor above the foyer, a café-restaurant was to be found with its own separate entrance from outside as well as an entrance within the cinema. The auditorium – 105 foot long and 72 foot wide at maximum – was spacious but unremarkable in design.

Letchworth resident Betty Miles started work at the Broadway as an usherette in 1945 and recalls: "We had a very smart commissionaire, very tall, who wore a long blue coat with gold braid and gold buttons on it. He would walk down the aisle spraying perfumed disinfectant and also would keep unruly children in order by banging a stick on his leg. Blackout curtains were still hanging at the front door at that time. There were a few seats fitted with a plug for a hearing aid. As an usherette, I would take the aid to be plugged into a socket. My job was also tear the tickets at the door and show patrons the way to their seats with a torch. The balcony was more tiring with lots of steps to climb. The balcony lounge was very nice with blue wicker chairs where one could sit and wait for the performance to start.

"After usheretting for about a year, I was offered a cashier's job in the box. My hours were slightly different. I started about 3 o'clock and finished at 9 o'clock – if the cash sheet tallied! Tax was 1½d, net 7½d, for a 9d ticket, so we had two columns on the sheet. We took the number of tickets at the start of the session and at the end. Tickets were 9d, 1/6, 2/-, 2/3 and 3/-. Booked seats were 3d

(top) The view towards the rear of the Broadway Letchworth in 1936.

(bottom) The main foyer of the Broadway Letchworth as attractively modernised in 1996. (September 1997 photograph by Allen Eyles.)

and 6d extra. The money for the booking fee was kept separate. Saturday was different – a lot of booked seats. The tickets were in a book – we had to stamp each ticket three times with the date and performance. We kept some back in case a mistake was made. There were separate performances starting at 2.30, 5.30 and 8.15. Most seats were booked if there was good film – a lot of them

by phone. The manager wore evening dress and everyone looked smart on a Saturday night. I worked from 10am until 9.30pm with one hour for lunch and one hour for tea. We were open for bookings. The small ticket office where I worked consisted of a chair, stool and switchboard – one line to the projection room, one to two separate offices and one to the Palace down the road. There was a phone and the ticket machine. The machine had four buttons. For one ticket, the lever was pressed down. For more than one ticket, the button was pressed once and then the lever. On the other side of the box there was a window where patrons would come to book seats. We used to start off with a £9 float for tickets. When a white £5 note with black writing was received, we had to take it to the manager to check. I also would go the Palace cinema for the Saturday morning shows for children – they would come to the cash desk with a handful of pennies, farthings and halfpennies for a 9d. ticket."

In 1955, the proscenium was widened and its height reduced to fit a CinemaScope screen, with 2ft of brickwork being cut away on each side. Hugh E. Bidwell, a director of the owning company (Letchworth Cinemas Ltd) and son of the late William Bidwell (whose partner had designed the Broadway in 1936), planned the architectural alterations which took place over two weeks at a cost of £8,000 and necessitated closing for only one evening's performances. In the early 1960s the Broadway was the scene of occasional live concerts with Chris Barber's Jazz Band and the Chas McDevitt Skiffle Group being recalled as performing there. A small extension was built at the rear of the building as a dressing room for visiting artistes and musicians. This was subsequently demolished.

In later years, alternate rows of seats

The largest auditorium at the Broadway Letchworth since it was tripled, using the original balcony. (September 1997 photograph by Allen Eyles.)

were removed from the stalls to give more leg room while the side walls of the circle and front stalls were curtained over. Unlike most large cinemas, the Broadway did not close its stalls area nor divide the auditorium into additional screens but just carried on the way it was, although consideration was given to continuing in the circle only and putting the stalls area to other uses. "The Broadway often runs at a loss but its owner, Miss Thomas, an active 80-year-old, has other profitable interests that allow her to subsidise the cinema which is her first love," noted John Benzing in the Cinema Theatre Association's *Bulletin* (September/October 1989).

Its long-term survival seemed doubtful – even though a 1990 proposal for a five-screen cinema as part of a new leisure centre went nowhere – but attempts to have it become a listed building in 1990 failed when the Department of the Environment concluded that it was of "insufficient interest, either historically or architecturally". Pleasant though the building was (and is), it is hard to criticise this finding.

Matters came to a head with the impending arrival of the Stevenage multiplex. Rather than give up or just carry on and hope for the best, the owners (still the original company) decided to put up a fight. The cinema closed on Sunday 25 February 1996 for conversion to three screens, with an afternoon charity screening (linked to the Cinema 100 celebrations of the year) of the Will Hay comedy, *Windbag the Sailor*. Over £2 million was spent on converting the cinema to a three-screen operation to the plans of London architects McFarlane Latter (who are also the designers of superior multiplexes at Mansfield and Wester Hailes, Edinburgh). The cost was met by a partnership between the cinema and the local authority through the Letchworth Garden City Heritage Foundation.

The cinema was closed for over four months, re-opening on 12 July 1996, the same day that the multiplex made its debut in Stevenage. The time had been well used, and the cinema now looked totally refreshed with high quality fittings and no hint of compromise on cost. The exterior was cleaned up – the stains disappeared from the stonework around the windows, a new, more prominent canopy was installed (the 1936 canopy had long vanished) and a stylish new Broadway sign replaced the undistinguished old one while neon around the front windows draws attention to the building. The spacious octagonal foyer with its radiating beams in the ceiling was retained and smartened up, returning to its original colours, the surviving art deco light fittings were restored at the top of the central pillar on alternating facets while the compass-style pattern in the floor surrounding it was retained. If this space seemed perhaps a little austere, the three auditoria looked very smart and plush, offering a most comfortable atmosphere with their predominant use of a relaxing green, reinforced by staff uniforms with green tops.

The balcony was re-stepped to provide more space and could hold 488 in luxury seats with multiplex-style drink holders, the back row having double 'love' seats. The side walls were curtained over and a new screen with generously gathered, side-opening curtains was placed in front. The screen size remained the same as before – 36 foot wide. The stepped edges which reduce the ceiling height at the side walls were from the old ceiling, but the centre section was covered in black tiles placed on grids running diagonally. Two art deco fittings over the side exits were retained from the original auditorium. A new, lower projection room was installed at the back.

The two downstairs auditoria seated 176 and 174, placed side by side in the stalls with a straight dividing wall between them. This inevitably made the auditoria asymmetrical with an inwardly curving wall on the outer side. The same decorative scheme and treatment, with art deco lights, was applied as upstairs but there was a regrettable absence of curtains in front of the screens. All three cinemas were equipped with Dolby stereo sound. Although the Broadway has remained at a disadvantage with only three screens compared with the twelve at Stevenage, it has survived the coming of the multiplex and remains open in 2002.

POTTERS BAR

Monday 8 October 1934

Ritz

Darkes Lane (corner of Byng Drive)

Built at the northern end of the lesser of the two main streets (the other being the High Street), the Ritz was one of many 1930s cinemas designed in a similar style by architect Major W. J. King. Others were at Edgware, Bowes Road (Southgate), Neasden, Turnpike Lane (Harringay), Hounslow West, Whitton and Park Royal. In the early 1930s Major King's buildings usually opened as part of the major ABC circuit, and the Potters Bar Ritz was no exception. What did make it different, however, is that, for reasons which are no longer clear, ABC leased and operated the Ritz for only a few months – seemingly until 2 March 1935, and certainly no later than the end of April 1935.

The Ritz was a super cinema in everything but size – it seated a fairly modest 1,170. Externally, its tower originally had a flashing light and the front was outlined in red neon. At the rear a floodlit car park provided space for 200 vehicles as well as a shed for bicycles. Three shops were attached to the development. There was a dance hall and tea lounge. In the auditorium, a 7 rank 2 manual British-made Compton organ was to be found, as well as a 20ft deep stage (the proscenium width was 40ft). Three dressing rooms were provided. The auditorium was illuminated by indirect lighting in the central dome and upwards from troughs by the proscenium arch in a changing colour scheme. The opening souvenir programme boasted: "While the building is designed and deco-rated on modern lines, there is little therein which may be called 'American jazz'." The walls and ceiling were covered in a material called Plastocrete. Major King's cinemas tended to become rather gloomy and oppressive as the years passed and the walls darkened from the dust and cigarette smoke – rather like sitting in a large cavern. Some of that "American jazz" would not have gone amiss but Major King was in his mid-fifties when this Ritz opened and clearly did not favour modern trends (although he had collaborated on "atmospheric" cinemas at Golders Green and Edgware when that style was the fashion).

The Potters Bar Ritz opened with Eddie Cantor's *Roman Scandals* supported by *One is Guilty*, a programme which ran for the rest of the week with an organ interlude and the Pathé Super Sound Gazette. The programme generally changed twice a week with matinées on Mondays, Thursdays and Saturdays. While part of the ABC circuit, the Ritz had ready access to good new films but once ABC withdrew it became an independent that had to play films after the cinemas in larger nearby towns like Barnet. At least it was spared competition in Potters Bar itself, although Odeon acquired a site locally (no plans seem to have been submitted and the land was sold during the 1950s).

The Ritz was built next to housing and by June 1935 local residents were up in arms complaining of the intrusive floodlights of the car park, the sound of the organ playing its signature tune and the national anthem, the hissing noise of the air purifying plant and the disturbances from youths drawn to the area – all of which was marshalled into an argument for a rates reduction.

For a couple of years after ABC's withdrawal, the Ritz was operated by Major King himself. The stage facilities were sometimes used, as when Potters Bar Dramatic Society

The Ritz Potters Bar just prior to its 1934 opening.

presented *The Sport of Kings* in April 1937. During that year, it was leased out to become part of the JHL group of cinemas formed by J. H. Lundy, former director of construction at Union Cinemas (this also included the Dominion East Barnet in 1943).

The family of James C. Robertson moved from Islington, north London, to Potters Bar a few weeks before the fall of France in mid-1940. He recalls: "I think my parents must have considered me too young to go as far afield as Barnet when we first arrived at Potters Bar, for my first cinematic memories in the area are of the Ritz, which was considered rather posh. It was quite common to have to queue to see a film, and as time

went on, I used to arrange to meet my pals inside pretty often. In retrospect, we must have been something of a nuisance to the adults in the audience, for I distinctly remember that the usherettes patrolled down the aisles and occasionally flashed their torches on us, presumably as a warning to keep quiet. Once I started going to the Barnet cinemas, the Ritz was less attractive as I had often already seen the main film, although one could sometimes get in free by the simple expedient of climbing through the male lavatory window at the side of the building. Nevertheless, I never entirely stopped going to the Ritz before I married and moved away from the area in October 1952. The films I particularly remember seeing there were the 1939 *Hound of the Baskervilles* as a B feature, *49th Parallel*, *Went the Day Well*, and a Soviet feature

The auditorium of the Ritz Potters Bar with the Compton organ console in full view.

about nurses at the front called *Natasha*, a film I have never seen since."

After the war, the Ritz was managed locally again. In November 1950 it was advertised in the film trade press for sale at £45,000 or for lease. In February 1953, Major King let it out to D. Oswald David and family, trading as Mayfield Cinemas, with Mr David personally managing it.

The Ritz fell on difficult times. Besides playing films much later than Barnet and other nearby towns, it had to contend with road widening and the construction of a new railway bridge (originally promised for 1938) which stopped buses passing the front doors as well as a severe winter for which the cinema's heating system was no longer adequate. The Ritz lost an average of £50 per week and the Urban District Council gained an order for the compulsory winding up of Mayfield Cinemas because of rates arrears amounting to £390. Although said to be

making a profit following a reduction in the rate of Entertainments Tax, the Ritz was forced to close in April 1954.

The building was returned to Major King by the Official Receiver. King complained bitterly about the fact that other cinemas – the nearest of which was 4.2 miles away – had made the Ritz show films at least three weeks later than they did. He spent nearly £10,000 on refurbishing the cinema, putting in new heating and ventilation and installing CinemaScope, proposing only to re-open it when these restrictive bars were lifted.

In fact, the Ritz was leased by George Snazelle and resumed operating from 24 January 1955 with the CinemaScope comedy *How to Marry a Millionaire* three weeks after its run at East Barnet. It seems to have been in difficulties again before long and to have reverted once more to the direct control of Major King, who recruited a particularly able and live-wire manager, Frank Seymour. From 1955 onwards, it gained access to the ABC circuit release at the same time as north-west London, Barnet and St Albans, and, if a particular programme did not seem too promising, a specialised booking or a belated run of the rival Odeon release was substituted. On 6 April 1956, Fess Parker, star of Disney's *Davy Crockett*, made a personal appearance in the afternoon prior to a week's run of the film. The most popular attraction ever to play the Ritz was apparently *The Ten Commandments* on an extended run. From 1963, live wrestling was introduced once a month on otherwise slack Monday evenings and the stage reverberated to occasional live beat shows.

Then, on 20 December 1965, Major King died at the age of 87. The executors kept the Ritz going while they offered it to the leading circuits – none was prepared to buy it outright, although an offer to purchase it in instalments was made by one smaller group. The cinema was trading at a profit but it was in poor condition and needed considerable renovation. In the absence of a satisfactory buyer, Tesco was granted an option to buy the Ritz in April 1967 and had an outline application for a new supermarket approved two months later. The Ritz then closed suddenly on Saturday 1 July 1967 following a week's run of the Morecambe and Wise comedy *That Riviera Touch* supported by a revival of a James Stewart American Civil War drama, *Shenandoah*.

There was considerable uproar locally at closure of the Ritz, and Tesco responded by offering to include a 500-600 seat cinema in the redevelopment if the council would lease the auditorium or guarantee the lessee. A petition with 6,238 names was delivered to the Minister of Housing and Local Government in Whitehall asking him to reverse the planning approval granted to Tesco. The Minister refused. Tesco then approached the major circuits about including a new cinema and found no interest. A building licence was obtained and the Ritz went under the wreckers' ball.

The Compton organ was saved and installed at Cheshunt Organs, 23 College Road, Cheshunt (almost adjacent to the site of the old Central Cinema). It was on view to customers at the rear of the shop and often played, both during normal hours and on Sunday open days.

Tesco's huge store in grey brick replaced the Ritz – a drab example of 1960s architecture. At the rear of the site beyond the car park there is a reminder of the old cinema in the name of Ritz Court, a group of houses around a small green.

From 1979, films were presented at Oakmere House (with 165 seats) on a part-time basis. Since then they have moved, still on a part-time basis, to the Wyllyotts Centre in Darkes Lane, which seats 425 (Oakmere House is now the Out and Out restaurant). Tesco has also moved on, its store on the site of the Ritz having become the Sports Academy leisure centre and the Dreams Bed Superstore.

RADLETT

Thursday 5 September 1929

Cinema

22 Watling Street

The Radlett Cinema was a conversion of the parish hall for regular cinema use by a local company. It opened with *Legion of the Condemned* to an almost full house (it had 300 seats) and the silent film had an orchestral music accompaniment played on a gramophone. The policy for this village cinema was to show films from Thursday to Saturday and reserve the other days for live events like concerts. Although it soon became essentially a full-time cinema, its stage and three dressing rooms were put to occasional use for amateur theatrical productions by groups such as the St Christopher Players. Programmes changed Sundays, Mondays and Thursdays and films were shown many weeks after Watford.

Late in the war the Cinema was part of a circuit eventually known as London and Provincial, which also ran the Publix Stevenage and Regal Standon in Hertfordshire. From July 1960 it closed on Sundays, Mondays and Thursdays and presented two changes of programme weekly – one on Tuesday and Wednesday, the other on Friday and Saturday. This attempt to survive quickly proved ineffective as the final show was on Saturday 27 August 1960, consisting of the British comedy *Bottoms Up* plus *The Rawhide Trail*.

In 1985 the building had been renamed the Radlett Hall and was run by Aldenham Parish Council for all types of functions. By 2002, it had become the Radlett United Synagogue.

RICKMANSWORTH

circa May 1912

Electric Picture Playhouse / Electric Palace

105 High Street

The old Town Hall was turned into a cinema with capacity for 300 people. In the tradition of the day, some variety acts were interspersed with the films. R. Barnett was an early proprietor but in later years it was run as the Electric Palace by A. Smith and his French wife (see picture on next page).

Although plans were deposited in 1913 for a rival Phoenix Theatre on the Uxbridge Road in the Mill End area, this remained the town's only cinema until the Picture House opened and put it out of business in 1927. Nearly sixty years later, local resident Wally Wilson still remembered what a blow this was to youngsters as the Electric Palace had seats for tuppence while the cheapest seats at the Picture House were sixpence!

The front of the building is boldly identified as 'The Old Town Hall' in 2002 with a florist and bakers to each side of a recessed entrance leading to old-fashioned doors. However, the upper storey has been completely removed and levelled off in plain brickwork while the central doors lead to the modern offices of Nicholson GDA and it seems that the entire rear of the building has been replaced.

The Electric Picture Playhouse Rickmansworth is seen circa 1912 at left. (See Previous page.)

Saturday 12 March 1927

Picture House

1 High Street

The Picture House was an enterprise by a group of local businessmen and it was designed by a firm of architects and surveyors called Morlands and built by Kempster and Williams. The cinema was sited alongside the railway embankment, some distance from the town centre, and until 1962, when modern lighter trains were introduced, the building was apt to vibrate as the steam trains went by, disturbing the mood when intimate scenes were unfolding on the screen.

The front of the Picture House was designed in a half-timbered Tudor style to blend in with the old town. There was a ballroom and tea lounge on the first floor overlooking the High Street. The auditorium was originally decorated in "black, flame and grey" and there was a coat of arms as well as gold-painted cherubs on the proscenium arch. At the back, there was a small, cantilevered balcony. Unfortunately, no photographs of the auditorium have come to light. Precise seating figures are available only from February 1943 when the balcony held 178 and the stalls 519, making a total of 697.

The new cinema opened on a Saturday afternoon with *Nell Gwyn*, a British costume spectacular starring Dorothy Gish, plus *Up In Mabel's Room*. Footage of the local Berkeley Hunt was also shown. There were no less than five different prices of admission: 6d, 1/1d, 1/6d, 1/10d, and 2/4d. Children were admitted from 4d with reduced prices at all shows except Saturday evenings. Programmes seem to have changed mid-week with matinées on Wednesdays and Saturdays.

An orchestra accompanied the silent films until 1930 when the Western Electric sound system was introduced. Tea dances were often held in the afternoon and patrons would combine them with a visit to the film show in the evening.

The Picture House Rickmansworth in 1927. (Courtesy of G. T. Rhodes and Wally Wilson.)

In 1933, the original group of proprietors gave up running the Picture House themselves and started leasing it out. It became part of the substantial Southan Morris circuit, SM Super Cinemas, around 1942. Eileen Rogers, who lived in Rickmansworth as a teenager from 1947, recalls: "I visited the Odeon and the Picture House. The latter was considered the scruffy one – which, of course, the children preferred. If the film was an 'A' certificate, children often asked adults to take them in."

The Picture House passed to the Essoldo circuit on 26 August 1954 when that group acquired S.M.'s interests. The cinema generally played the weekly ABC circuit release and easily outlasted the Odeon. But Essoldo decided against renewing the lease on the Picture House in 1963, resulting in its closure on 22 June at the end of a week's run of the Bette Davis-Joan Crawford shocker, *What Ever Happened to Baby Jane?*

After standing unused for a while, it was sold and gutted, becoming a factory making Venetian blinds and hanging baskets until 1979. A property company then wanted to demolish it and erect a new building. The local planning authority insisted on the building and its mock-Tudor front remaining. However, architects Rolfe Judd Group Practice of London were allowed to hang reddish-orange tiles at first floor level across the frontage and along the side walls. The old exits on the corners of the frontage were blocked in and large windows introduced on the ground floor. Externally, the building never looked like a cinema and it became only recognisable in its basic shape as the same structure but it was a pleasant and commendable adaptation. Internally, no trace of its cinema past remained. In 2002, the building is occupied on the ground floor by the Watford and Three Rivers National Health Service Primary Care Trust and on the first floor by Coexis.

Wednesday 29 January 1936

Odeon

93/95 High Street

This was the only Odeon in Hertfordshire developed by the circuit until the Hemel Hempstead Odeon was built in 1960. (The North Watford and Barnet Odeons were taken over during construction; other Odeons were cinemas acquired years after opening.) The Rickmansworth theatre was designed by the Andrew Mather practice, one of the principal architectural firms that planned new Odeons. It was the first of thirty-three new Odeons that opened in 1936. The cinema itself cost £15,869 to build

The Odeon Rickmansworth at opening in 1936. The shop in the adjacent parade at right has yet to be let.

and the adjacent shops and flats, called Odeon Parade, added another £4,655. A car park seems to have been provided at the rear with an exit onto Talbot Road.

The site, between the High Street and the town stream, was so waterlogged that an elaborate system of piling was required. The frontage is reported to have been re-designed in a more traditional manner with brick and stone dressings to blend with the area and gain planning approval, with urns mounted on the parapet and two different bas-relief panels of reclining females above the side exits. There was a very shallow canopy over the entrance because of the narrow pavement and the front edge was decorated with swags at each end. Although lacking the streamlining and expanse of buff tiles that defined the celebrated Odeon style, the cinema had a tower to advertise its whereabouts with name signs in the distinc-tive trademark lettering on each side as well as on the main frontage. Neon was used on the name signs and to decorate the frontage at night. Curiously, the adjacent shops and flats of Odeon Parade were built to a lower height and in a different, more modern style curving round the corner into Church Street.

The Odeon had a large foyer with bold, directional stripes in the rubber flooring and art deco light fittings in the ceiling. The auditorium was designed on the stadium principle with the balcony being a raised rear section rather than overhanging the stalls. There were 920 seats – 574 in the stalls, 346 in the balcony. The principle source of illumination was the lighting around the edge of the rectangular recess in the ceiling, supplemented by fountain-style wall lights and the stage footlights. A novel touch was the art-deco style radiator grilles below the wall lights. Strongly decorated grilles sloped inwards to the proscenium opening which was more a space in the end wall than a decorated feature in its own right. This was the first of a few Odeons that eliminated the orchestra rail: seating was increased by bringing the front row much closer to the curtains. (Although new cinemas had little or no use for orchestra pits, they were usually included to fill in the space.)

The opening was delayed for two days by the death of King George V. The inaugural film was *On Wings of Song*, starring Grace Moore, and for the opening night's invited audience the orchestra of Miss Dewey and her Savoy Ladies appeared, although for the rest of the week another film called *Unknown Woman* was shown.

There was no café but teas were served at the Odeon for many years. Apparently the Odeon shared the Gaumont British newsreel with the Picture House, requiring rapid movement at times between the two buildings to keep to the programme schedules.

The Odeon was never a big moneymaker and receded in significance six months after opening when the Odeon circuit took over and renamed the Plaza in Watford. In later years it trailed well behind the Watford and North Watford Odeons in obtaining films and keen cinemagoers did not wait for them to turn up locally. Programmes were generally changed midweek and by 1956 even the Wednesday matinée had been dropped with a 5pm opening daily except for Saturday afternoon.

The Odeon was one of fifty-nine cinemas closed by the Rank Organisation in a purge of chronic money-losers on the Odeon and Gaumont circuits in the autumn and winter of 1956. After many weeks of rumours, the final decision to shut the Rickmansworth building was apparently taken on 17 December 1956 and it closed after the Christmas holidays on Saturday 5 January

(top) The foyer of the Odeon Rickmansworth in 1936 has a display at back right, listing the other Odeons to date and showing the circuit chief Oscar Deutsch.

(bottom) The auditorium of the Odeon Rickmansworth in 1936 showing the raised rear section.

1957 with *The Mountain* starring Spencer Tracy supported by *The Big Tip-Off*. It was only a few weeks short of its twenty-first anniversary.

The property was put up for sale and eventually purchased by the Urban District Council which contemplated turning it into a public hall and indoor swimming pool before deciding to pull it down in 1965. Its site was turned into a car park by the summer. The former auditorium area is still used for this purpose in 1985 but a plain office block has been erected on the front section in red brick that fails to match the surviving parade of shops and flats (this was for many years Union Carbide House but is vacant in early 2002). The adjacent shops and flats still form part of Odeon Parade in 2002.

In time, the need for a new entertainment centre became evident but by then it was too late to save the Odeon or Picture House. Instead, the new and attractive Watersmeet Centre was built across the road from where the Odeon had been. It opened on 1 May 1975 and films are shown part of the time in the 390-seat auditorium.

Crowds gather at the fire which permanently closed the Royston Cinema in 1933 (the roof of the auditorium is missing). (Courtesy of Margaret Shepherd.)

ROYSTON

Tuesday 1 July 1913

Cinema
1 Priory Lane

The Cinema was built in six weeks opposite the police station. The original proprietor was Mr Hatrick (the former Bishop's Stortford cinema manager who was involved in the Hoddesdon Cinema opened earlier in 1913). This building had a stucco front and a hanging 2,000-candle electric arc lamp. The auditorium, 28ft wide by 90ft long, accommodated 400 patrons on a sloping floor. There was a rear projection throw of 26ft onto the back of the screen which put the nearest exit 40ft away in case of fire when an iron shutter would close the porthole in the brick-built operating box.

Fires had caused fatalities at cinemas and safety was of considerable concern. In fact, the Royston Cinema suffered at least two fires. In October 1913 the projectionist dropped a red-hot carbon he was removing with pliers; it fell on the re-wind table and 7,000 ft of film worth £100 was destroyed, but there was no audience panic and the manager had to persuade patrons to leave. Performances resumed the next day.

However, the other fire was devastating. At 1pm on Tuesday 13 June 1933, the Cinema was empty but for a kitten when fire (thought to be caused by faulty wiring) broke out and gutted the auditorium, with the roof collapsing within fifteen minutes. The films, the projector and the kitten were rescued.

The proprietor at this time, John R. Cox, was fully insured and he set about building the Priory Cinema to replace it. As a temporary measure, Cox hired the British Legion Hall in Mill Road, put in a projection box, and showed films six days a week from Thursday 29 June until the Priory was ready.

By 1985, a private house stood on the Cinema's site while the adjacent cottages seen in the photograph were still standing.

Monday 27 November 1933

Priory

Priory Lane
(corner with Newmarket Road)

The Priory Royston in 1933. (Courtesy of Margaret Shepherd.)

The opening film was *Cavalcade*, a smash hit of the year. There were some 600 seats in stalls and balcony priced from 9d to 2/4d. Seats from 1/3d upwards were bookable and there was a free car park. The cinema (architect: E.B. Parkinson of Cambridge) was only one part of John Cox's new enterprise. Alongside he built the Green Plunge open-air swimming pool which opened at 3pm on 5 July 1934 and stayed open until the end of September when the weather became too cold. A café was attached to the pool entrance and this was open all year from October 1934 onwards. It was an early example of a varied leisure centre and the manager of the cinema was also responsible for the pool where admission was originally 1/- except for Sundays (1/6d) with a special 3d admission between 7 and 8 am.

There was, at one point in the 1940s, a fire at the Priory and the cinema became an early exponent of No Smoking which had the benefit of giving a much clearer picture and making a light decoration scheme feasible. The Priory remained a Cox enterprise until the 1970s (the Regal and Empire Biggleswade were also Cox theatres) and the almost inevitable flirtation

with bingo occurred. It took place on Thursdays, Fridays and Saturdays from 31 March 1977 reducing films (beginning with *Jaws*) to the first four days of the week (*Jaws* played two abbreviated weeks).

Then Brian Horsley of Cranbrook took over and returned the Priory to full-time cinema – *Saturday Night Fever* began its new lease of life running the full seven days starting Sunday 23 April 1978. There was normally one show nightly except for two shows on Sunday. The no smoking rule had been abandoned by this time and the cinema came under the same ownership as the Broadway Letchworth. In November 1983, it was taken over, initially on an eight-year lease, by Des and Margaret Shepherd and by Bob Lee whose primary business interest was Sheplee Electrical behind the cinema. However, Margaret Shepherd had been an usherette at the cinema and her father was a projectionist there.

The Priory became a rare small-town survivor. It seated 305 and benefited from improved seats, carpets and curtains obtained from the Welwyn Embassy when that closed. Although it has never been of great architectural interest (which has pre-

The disappointingly plain auditorium of the Priory Royston, seen from the balcony in 2000. No photograph showing the original proscenium arch has been located. (Photograph by Allen Eyles.)

The sunburst pattern on the doors and in the stained glass above, and the art deco light fitting at the entrance to the Priory Royston in 2000. (Photograph by Allen Eyles.)

However, it closed on Thursday 28 September 2000 with *Stuart Little*.

The owners originally declared that the cinema would be leased to another operator but after several months a campaign was started to get it re-opened by a local group called FLICS – Film Lovers Independent Cinema Support – founded and chaired by a former cinema manager, Nick Holliday. After eleven months, Holliday reported: " We have been offered a short-term lease and are considering several options. This little gem is in lovely art deco style – not glamorous but homely. Somehow it escaped the 1970s demise of some of our lovely shows. It is part of an early example of a leisure centre. The site consists of an open-air swimming pool still in use – the pool/cinema café is now an Indian restaurant. Unfortunately the site owners wish to develop the site and we can only get the offer of a one-year lease. The capital outlay would be hard to recoup within twelve months." One problem was that a significant amount of work needed to be undertaken before the cinema could re-open. At least one potential saviour emerged and more than one re-opening date came and went. Sadly, Nick Holliday died after a short illness, North Herts District Council had its request for "spot listing" turned down after English Heritage advised against it, and a demolition crew was hard at work in mid-August.

vented it from being listed), it remained an excellent example of a well-run independent cinema. After nearly seventeen years, the Shepherds announced their retirement and a campaign started to keep the cinema going. Five hundred people signed a petition organised by a local councillor.

ST ALBANS

Monday 27 July 1908

Alpha / Poly / Regent

166 London Road

The Alpha Picture Palace was the first permanent cinema in Hertfordshire. It was in the upper part of a building and on the ground floor there was a restaurant, hairdressing salon and public baths. The cinema was part of the activities of the Alpha Trading Company whose managing director was Arthur Melbourne-Cooper. The company scripted and shot films under contract for other organisations (who submitted the basic idea or storyline) and its works, offices, studios and outdoor shooting space reputedly covered nearly two acres. The site of the studios is marked by a 'Cinema 100' plaque (celebrating the first hundred of years of public cinema in Britain) placed on the wall of Telford Court in Alma Road, which is on the other side of London Road from the cinema.

The cinema, with its subsidiary halls,

The Alpha St. Albans in 1909 with wooden forms nearest screen, chairs nearest camera. Note the uncurtained screen with rounded corners. The rear section does not look raised. (Courtesy of Kevin S. Wheelan.)

was used for indoor work during the day and opened to the public for shows in the evening. A profile of the Alpha company in *The Bioscope* (18 September 1908) observes: "It has a seating capacity of 800, and a feature worthy of note is that the lower priced places are in front and the better ones at the back. This arrangement was somewhat resented at first by the patrons of the higher priced seats, but when they found that the specially-raised floor gave them a better view than could be got from the front, they appreciated the innovation. The operator's 'box' does not stand in the usual place inside the auditorium. It is a roomy apartment built out as an annexe, and therefore affords immunity from accident as well as from interference by the public. There are also an operator's room and manager's office. Altogether a very convenient and attractive hall."

In a 1967 article, Melbourne-Cooper's daughter, Audrey Wadowska, noted: "Beside the paybox were phials of perfume (Pivor of

Paris) from which the ladies could spray their handkerchiefs. Perfumed cards were also distributed. Cadburys contracted to supply the confectionery, and boxes of chocolates were specially made with the name 'Alpha Picture Palace' embossed in gold on a red background. Prices were twopence, fourpence and sixpence and free teas were provided for patrons during the matinées. At the rear of the cinema hall were eight boxes – plush curtained and tastefully furnished with two chairs and a table – which could be reserved in advance for two shillings and sixpence. Comfortable tip-up seats were provided in all parts of the house (except the tuppennys) and an imposing proscenium was designed and executed by Fred Karno, of music hall fame. 'Boots' Martin, an ex-guardsman, was the first commissionaire, dressed in claret and gold uniform, and there were also three 'chocolate boys' in green and gold uniforms purchased from Cadburys after use at the Paris exhibition. A policeman was engaged nightly to deal with the rough element. A large banner was strung across the road outside the cinema advertising the programme, and a man-lifting box-kite carrying advertising matter was also used during the daytime. The kite was subsequently purchased by Gordon Selfridge, for use in advertising his new store."

In January 1910 the new safety provisions of the Cinematograph Act came into effect and a licensing officer's report on 31 October of that year refers to the Alpha: "I have had to insist that the whole building shall be remodelled, its present condition being such that it is surprising that it has been allowed to be used as a place of public entertainment." In June 1910, plans had been drawn up and submitted by local architect Percival Blow for Melbourne-Cooper and these were carried out to deal

with the criticisms. The basement and ground floor now contained workshops, the ground floor also had shops along with a new entrance and the cinema remained at first floor level.

It became the Poly from 20 April 1918 onwards. It seems to have been reconstructed to plans of Percival Blow in 1923, to turn the ground floor into a stalls area seating 573 with a balcony for 314 and boxes at the rear. It was re-named the Regent from 2 October 1926 and boasted a full orchestra to accompany the silent films and a grand organ. By this time a Palais de Dance had been established in the basement.

Fire broke out in the early hours of Thursday 15 December 1927. The alarm was sounded at 3.26am and the fire brigade arrived in minutes to battle for three hours against the dense smoke and a blinding snowstorm. The ceiling collapsed, the café was soaked, the dance hall submerged in water, the entire front of the building including the projection box destroyed and only the organ appeared to be undamaged. The probable cause was a lighted cigarette. The site was cleared and the new Capitol cinema opened there in 1931.

Saturday 20 January 1912

Cinema / Chequers

24 Chequer Street

The St Albans Cinema was erected in just seven weeks by builders Ezra Dunham working night and day. It replaced Adey and White's Brewery and was designed by local architect Henry F. Mence. This was the only cinema in the heart of the town. (It almost had an early rival when some kind of portable building of corrugated iron was erected in Hatfield Road on capital of £200 by one Russell Edwards whose architect, a Mr Hubbard, received advice from Henry F. Mence, architect of the Chequers. In August 1913, a licence for cinema use was refused and Mr Edwards was sued by his partner, Thomas Swan, over the alleged misappropriation of £5 15s 7d.)

There were 799 seats on a single sloping floor, according to the plans, and the hall was 36ft wide by 90ft 3ins long. The walls were of brick, the floor of cement, and there was no wood anywhere that might catch fire while the carpet was made of *paper* that was claimed to be fire and damp proof. The colour scheme was a rose tint and the seats all tipped-up while even the threepennys were cushioned. The entrance was between two shops and there was Tudor-style decoration above. It was said that the building might later be turned into a proper theatre with a new front, and space had been reserved for a stage and dressing rooms.

An embarrassing start occurred when the opening was held up while electrical adjustments were made to satisfy the authorities but the Cinema soon became a popular part of St Albans' life. In January 1927 it was acquired by Captain Frederick A. Webb (see Harpenden) and renamed the Chequers. In January 1928 it played the silent version of *Ben-Hur* for a fortnight and claimed that 12,791 people had seen it in the first week – adding that this was more than the total population of St Albans according to the 1921 census!

Early in 1933 the cinema was extended at the screen end into the space originally reserved for a possible stage and the seating increased to around 1,000. By the late 1940s it regularly played the lucrative ABC release programme of the week and when it also had access to the CinemaScope films on the independent Fourth or Fox circuit in the 1950s it was well placed to survive the cold

winds of change in exhibition.

But in 1962 the Chequers was purchased by a property company for conversion into a supermarket and closed on Saturday 30 June after a week's run of two revivals, *Young in Heart* plus *The Charge at Feather River*. Planning permission was refused for the change, both locally and on appeal to Whitehall – the Minister of Housing declared that such an extensive change would be premature as a comprehensive redevelopment scheme for the entire area was pending. The thwarted owners granted a year's lease (with an option to renew) to Panton Film Distributors who, after redecoration and reseating, re-opened the Chequers on Saturday 1 December 1962 with the film *The 300 Spartans*.

Its five months of closure had been long enough for the ABC release to pass to the St Albans Gaumont and the Chequers was forced to revive old films or play minor new releases as the only other major weekly release went into the Odeon. The Chequers often played 'split weeks' (changing its pro-

The Chequers St. Albans in June 1962 just before its first closure. (© St. Albans Museums.)

gramme on Thursdays) but fought back with big advertisements in the press. It was a losing battle and after a six-day run of a typical revival programme, *Last Train from Gun Hill* plus *Escape from Zahrain*, the Chequers had a one-day booking of *Portrait of a Mobster* plus *His Majesty O'Keefe* on Sunday 18 July 1965 before closing to become the first total conversion of a cinema to bingo in Hertfordshire from Friday 23 July 1965.

This proved a success but in 1974 the building was compulsorily purchased by the Council. The Chequers Bingo and Social Club transferred to the now closed Gaumont but, when demolition was delayed, some further limited use for bingo occurred here as well. In 1979 Panton even contemplated renting the building back to re-open it as a cinema but this idea fell through.

The building was adapted to form part of The Maltings development in 1983. The canopy and mock Tudor frontage vanished as its frontage was totally transformed into three shops with V-shaped projecting windows on the first floor while the passage that extended down the side of the cinema to the left has been filled in with a shop extension. The rear of the building has also been completely changed to create two storeys of shops and business premises in the pedestrian precinct behind.

Thursday 8 June 1922

Grand Cinema Palace / Grand Palace / Gaumont

Stanhope Road

The Grand Cinema Palace was located on the eastern edge of the town, on the other side of the main railway line, close to St Albans City station. It was designed by Harry R. Finn of local architects Mence and

Finn, the builders were T. Day and Son of Luton, and the cost was £35,000. The owning company was headed by George H. Whiting of St Albans. Unlike the Cinema, it took almost a year to construct. The Palace seated just under 1,100 in the stalls and 308 in the balcony – a total of 1,408. A stone portico of modest size made a dignified impression but did little to hide the brick bulk of the auditorium behind. There was an oak foyer with fireplace (where a large electric fire was installed) and a tea lounge on the mezzanine floor (teas were still served in the early 1950s). The auditorium was 130ft long and had a predominantly blue decorative scheme that extended to the colour of the velvet-covered seats, carpets, curtains and even the lighting. The building stretched back to Granville Street where there was a separate entrance to the front stalls and glass-covered queueing space. The screen was set l0 foot back on the stage. A 14-piece orchestra was provided to accompany the silent films and variety turns included in the programmes. There was a car park. The opening attraction was *Squibs*, a very popular British film of the period starring Betty Balfour.

In the late 1920s Alfred Lever took over

The Grand Palace St. Albans in 1922.

the Grand Palace (as it was now called), then
D. J. James acquired the cinema in the early
1930s, having some updating carried out in
1932. Around 1937, James' small chain of
cinemas, which also included the St Albans
Capitol, were taken over by General Cinema
Finance, in which J. Arthur Rank was a partner. A leading cinema architect, Leslie H.
Kemp, drew up plans for what would have
been a thorough modernisation of the
Grand Palace and a contract was placed in
August 1939 for the work to be carried out,
but the declaration of war on Germany early
the following month led to the scheme
being abandoned.

GCF became part of Odeon around
March 1943. This led to the opening of an
Odeon National Cinema Club for children
on Saturday mornings from 15 May 1943.
When the Odeon and Gaumont circuits
were merged administratively, the way was
open for the Grand Palace, which regularly
showed the weekly Gaumont circuit release,

*The auditorium of the Grand Palace St. Albans in
1922.*

to be called the Gaumont from Sunday 19
February 1950.

In 1959, a new release split gave the
Gaumont the inferior 'National' circuit programmes, and it was fortunate that, when
the Chequers closed for a while in 1962, the
cinema was able to take over the strong
weekly ABC circuit release and retain it after
the Chequers re-opened. Once the Odeon
(ex-Capitol) was tripled in early 1973 (by
which time the Chequers had taken up
bingo), almost all the best pictures were
channelled there and the Gaumont's days
were clearly numbered, although some
enterprising off-beat programming was
tried out. The Gaumont closed on Saturday
27 October 1973 after a week's run of *The
Man Called Noon* supported by a revival of

The Winners. It was sold to the Panton company for £62,000 in May 1974 and the Chequers Bingo Club moved there where it remained until August 1987. The building was demolished in 1988 although the fixtures and fittings, including the entrance pillars, were carefully removed for possible use elsewhere. It has been replaced by some of the flats in the development known as Chatsworth Court.

Thursday 3 December 1931

Capitol / Odeon

166 London Road

After the old Regent burned down, plans were first submitted for a new cinema on the site in February 1928 (architect: Percival Blow) with alterations and additions by J. Martin Hatfield in May 1929. Further plans were submitted by Hatfield in April 1930 and in 1931 and these became the basis for the Capitol. The decorative scheme was handled by another well-known cinema

The Odeon (ex-Capitol) St. Albans in 1949. (Courtesy of Derek Knights.)

architect, Robert Cromie, who may well have subcontracted the work to a specialist firm. Lou Morris promoted the venture, which provided for 1,620 seats (1,168 in the stalls, 452 in the balcony), a 20 foot deep stage, a Compton organ, a café, and three dressing rooms. The Capitol was built lengthways to the road and because of the sharp drop of the land it was entered, rather unusually, at circle level. On the London Road, the side wall was rendered and divided by pointed decorative towers and recessed panels for advertising. On the other side, the vast expanse of brick wall towered over and blighted Lower Paxton Road. There were several flights of steps down the side of the building at the screen end connecting Lower Paxton Road to London Road. By 1935, if not before, parking space for up to 500 cars had been provided off London Road almost opposite the cinema.

Lou Morris sold the Capitol very quickly and it became part of the D. J. James circuit, as did the Grand Palace. Mr James' architects, Kemp and Tasker, were brought in to enlarge the stalls to give a total seating capacity of 1,728. General Cinema Finance bought the James cinemas and later became part of Odeon, cueing a change of name to Odeon from the first week of January 1945. (Apparently, Odeon Theatres had earlier acquired a site in St Albans for a new cinema at Grange Gardens for which plans were interrupted by the war; no plans or announcements seem to have been made before the war and the site was not disposed of until 27 July 1960.)

In the early 1960s there were occasional one-day live shows, most of which seemed to feature Billy Fury, with other pop stars including Joe Brown, Karl Denver, John Leyton and Eden Kane.

In 1972 this became one of many cinemas on the circuit to undergo a simple

The auditorium of the Capitol (later Odeon) St. Albans in 1931 with its oddly faceted side walls and the organ console in its raised position.

tripling. The stalls were closed and two mini-cinemas created under the balcony while the circle remained open in the evening, using the existing screen. Work took six weeks and there was an open day on Saturday 20 January 1973 for the public to view the results. The following day, Odeon 1 (the old circle, seating 452 as it had on opening back in 1931) screened *A Clockwork Orange*, Odeon 2 (115 seats) showed *Butterflies are Free* plus *And Now for Something Completely Different*, and Odeon 3 (129 seats) presented *Nicholas and Alexandra*.

The Odeon was extensively refurbished around late 1988 when the cinema in the former balcony was briefly closed so that a new screen could be erected just in front of the seats and the disused front stalls area

converted into a fourth cinema with its screen in the lower part of the original proscenium arch. A coffee shop called Oscars was introduced, accessible from both the street and the foyer, and a bar for the exclusive use of patrons was opened.

As the only cinema in a large town, the Odeon remained very popular and had been considerably smartened up, at least externally, when its closure was announced for Sunday 20 August 1995. This was in an attempt to persuade cinemagoers to support the circuit's new multiplex at Hemel Hempstead which would open five days later. An Odeon marketing executive, Stuart

Francis was quoted in the local press as saying that the St Albans cinema was "trading quite comfortably" while an independent circuit reported that Rank was not interested in leasing it to anyone else. A vigorous Save Our Cinema campaign, organised by local residents Lynette Warren and Dave Byatt, was launched a few weeks before the closure and the Council opened negotiations with Odeon to delay or cancel the shutdown – but to no avail. Apparently, Odeon did suggest that, if the Council would buy the building at the asking price of £800,000, the company would run it as a cinema in exchange for a management fee. The Council seemed more interested in persuading another cinema operator to build elsewhere. *Sunday Times* columnist Peter Kellner weighed in on 6 August: "The Odeon is a friendly place, within easy reach of more than 50,000 people. It has introduced my three- and five-year-olds to the joys of cinema. My teenage children and their friends are regular customers. They do what Steven Norris, the transport minister, says they should do, and walk there. After August 20, that option will no longer be available. In its place the Rank Organisation is opening a multiplex on the edge of Hemel Hempstead, seven miles away. The only practical way to visit the cinema will be to take the car and pump more carbon monoxide into the air. […] If Rank's only concern is to maximise its return on capital, its strategic decision may well be right. It can probably make more profit from selling its St Albans site and investing the proceeds elsewhere. The same goes for so many shops and amenities in so many towns. The social damage may be enormous, the cumulative addition to pollution health-threatening, the pressure on our roads and countryside appalling – but the commercial arguments are compelling… the plight of our Odeon reflects on the overall quality of life in Britain today." Celebrities wrote in support of the campaign, including Emma Thompson: "It would be madness to close the St Albans Odeon – an act which only speaks contempt for the audience which keeps such companies as Rank afloat."

A protest was organised outside the cinema on its last day. Gerald Murphy, one of the performers in *Waterworld*, the last film shown on Screen One, turned up to lend his support. An attempt was made to have the cinema listed, although it had no great architectural merit and the campaign was more about having a cinema anywhere in St Albans than preserving the existing building.

The Odeon was stripped of its fixtures, fittings and equipment. The Council declined to buy the building, officers finding the asking price excessive in view of problems (real or potential) with damp, the state of the roof and subsidence.

The Council established a formal subcommittee, the Cinema Working Party, and wrote to potential operators in July 1997 about opening a new cinema elsewhere. Several showed interest and three possible locations were identified but progress proved difficult and a former Rank executive, Anthony Williams, now an independent consultant, was engaged in 1998 to write a fresh report. It concluded that there was scope for a five-screen niche cinema to complement the three multiplexes that were within a 20-minute drive time (at Hatfield, Watford and Hemel Hempstead). An investigation of nine possible sites was whittled down to one: a first floor area in The Maltings shopping centre. A marketing pack was circulated to fourteen potential operators, of which eight showed interest, but then there were delays emanating from the owner of the site. In June 1999, the Council decided to market the low, two-storey Civic Centre car park, in Bricket Road at the back of the Alban Arena, as a site for a new cinema complex along with restaurants and other leisure facilities. The structure seemed to have the advantage of foundations sufficiently deep for at least two additional storeys to be added, as well as being sited in the city centre rather than out of town: as a leisure centre, it could be entered on foot from the main shopping street, St Peter's Street, walking down the side of the Alban Arena.

A developer took on the site and came to an agreement with Cine-UK, operator of the Cineworlds at Stevenage and Bishop's Stortford, to lease space for an eight-screen multiplex after the company successfully insisted that all the auditoria should be on the same level. The external design of the scheme came in for heavy criticism, being described as a "Lego-block building" by the chairman of the local Civic Society in May 2001. In April 2002, the project had stalled with reports that the developer had pulled out because of rising costs. It seems that the existing foundations would not have supported the scale of development that was envisaged so that the entire site would have had to be cleared. It seems possible that the site might still host a smaller cinema development, perhaps attached to the Alban Arena.

The Alban Arena had opened as City Hall in 1969 and took its current name when it was later expanded with a new entrance. Long before the Odeon closed, some more specialised films had been shown as part of the programme of events at the 856-seat venue which has a flat main floor with retractable bleacher-style seating at the rear, and a balcony with side galleries (about 620 seats in all are at a suitable angle for viewing films). The Arena has continued to show films on many weekdays but not usually weekends, and has had to wait some months for prints to become available for the limited screening time it can offer around other events. It has both 16mm and 35mm projection facilities, Dolby surround sound and a large screen, with side and top masking opening to 28 feet wide by 12 feet high, which can be flown.

Meanwhile, in April 2002, the former Odeon looked in a sorry state, with much of the rendering on the frontage having come off. The building has been bought by Tesco, along with the car park opposite, but no plans had been submitted for its future use.

SAWBRIDGEWORTH

Thursday 5 February 1914

Cinema

Sayesbury Road
(corner of Sayesbury Avenue)

The Cinema was an enterprise of H. A. Roberts who had been responsible for the opening up of the Sayesbury housing estate and who was determined that Sawbridgeworth should have its own entertainment to keep the local population from going further afield. The Cinema's somewhat exotic facade was lit up at night by over seventy light bulbs; the entrance had marble facings and tiles; the auditorium seated 400; and the whole structure was erected in little more than two months. On adjoining open space, Mr Roberts planned to establish lawn tennis as well as show films in the open air. The opening programme, in the days before feature-length films had become properly established, consisted of three dramas (*Mysterious Club, Detective's Stratagem* and *A Strange Way*) plus three comedies (*Mabel's New Hero, Bidonia's Opportunity* and *Happy Dustmen*). During World War I, the cinema's projectionist was called up for active service and Jack Nash of Bishop's Stortford has recalled that his mother took the operator's place. She later ran the box-office and was a member of staff for the rest of the cinema's life while her husband took charge of the projection box, to be followed by his son.

By 1921 Mr Roberts had fallen from favour to such an extent that the Chief Constable opposed the licence being renewed as he was "not a fit person" to run the Cinema. It was taken over by G. W. and R. S. V. Sankey who were granted a licence from 11 November 1921. In 1930 the lessee was B. K. Parfitt – until July when the Cinema was bought by Ernest E. Smith who ran the nearby Bishop's Stortford Cinema and who put his son, G. P. A. Smith, in charge of managing both properties. By the late 1940s the Cinema was losing money as picturegoers preferred to see films earlier at more modern cinemas in bigger towns rather than wait for them to arrive at Sawbridgeworth. "It used to attract country people," recalled Eric Smith, another son of Ernest Smith, "but it was never very full."

Local historian Dorothy Cleal has vivid and affectionate memories of the place from the late 1930s and the Second World War period. Writing in *Hertfordshire Countryside* (March 2002), she recalls: "The building was about the size of a big village hall, and must have looked rather grand in its day, having a frontage that looked a bit like the Alamo – or, rather, a bit of theatrical scenery purporting to be the Alamo. (I think there was a brief fashion in things Spanish and Mexican in the era of its inception)… A visit to this delightful little cinema was a treat for the connoisseur. The seats, of faded red plush, were obviously original, and here and there an emerging spring made an overlong programme something of an endurance test. The back row was comprised of double seats, for the amorously inclined, giving rise to much ribaldry from the young. In the days when I was an enthusiastic patron the programme was usually changed twice a week, and there would be a double bill. If the 'B' picture wasn't very long there would also be a Silly Symphony (very popular) and a documentary which, for some reason, always seemed to be about coal mines. During the war there were delightful (in retrospect!) Ministry of Information shorts, about Using Your Handkerchief or Careless Talk Costing Lives. I suppose the

The showy frontage of the Sawbridgeworth Cinema. The Sawbridgeworth part of the name display was obliterated during World War II as part of a national policy of removing place names to avoid helping German parachutists, should they descend.

war years were The Cinema's heyday, as with all places of entertainment throughout the country. Perhaps our critical faculties were slightly dulled and we were hungry for a good laugh or a bit of escapist drama, but it seemed to me that we enjoyed everything – and when we did not, there were boos and catcalls in the manner of disapproving audiences since the days of the Romans. That in itself was part of the entertainment. The cinema's equipment wasn't, perhaps, of the best or most up-to-date, and had a tendency to break down, usually, of course, at the most poignant moment. The lights would go up (no subtle lighting here, just overhead bulbs, illuminating mercilessly the disarray in the back row)…

"I remember the smell, a unique combination of cinema disinfectant (dutifully sprayed during each performance), orange peel, tobacco smoke, human bodies, Californian Poppy, and, on at least one occasion

I recall, fish and chips. The evacuated mothers, adapting with difficulty to provincial life after an upbringing in Bethnal Green or Hackney, would take their place with the young, and perhaps sit through the programme twice, bringing along feeding bottles and other refreshments; once, as I say, I saw a full-scale fish supper in progress, complete with newspaper, soggy with vinegar, and smelling – I must admit – delicious…

"In addition to evacuees, a large proportion of the audience would be made up of servicemen, mostly airmen from the nearby base. In the dark days when invasion was a very real threat, many servicemen had to have their rifles with them at all times – but not, for obvious reasons, in places of public entertainment, so it was part of [projectionist] Mr. [Jack] Nash's job to relieve his customers of their weapons before they took their places in the auditorium. He then locked them up and reissued them when the show was over…

"The cinema had no car park – there was no need, and in any case, the building was approached by a narrow path or 'twitchell'. Patrons often came by bicycle, and there was a bike stand at the side. It was a fairly regular occurrence for a bike or two to be stolen, this perhaps not done with real malice aforethought so much as a need to get back to camp in a hurry…

"One final reminiscence. If an overlong programme necessitated a trip to the Ladies, this involved leaving the building and following a path round the side (no easy matter in the blackout), groping until one's hand found the curtain of ivy which concealed the door of the toilet. It may not have been the most luxurious of conveniences, but there can't have been many more picturesque."

The Cinema was the first victim in Hertfordshire of the post-war decline of the film industry. It closed on 2 May 1953 after a three-day run of David Lean's aerial drama *The Sound Barrier* plus a short. In November 1954, it was advertised as a "Valuable Freehold Building with over 2,000 square feet of Floor Space Suitable for Warehousing, Light Industry etc." It was announced for sale at public auction on Thursday 20 January 1955. In the event, it became the Catholic Church of the Most Holy Redeemer with an added porch and side extension and now very plain frontage. It is hard to imagine this building, now in a quiet, leafy residential side street, was once a cinema for forty years.

STANDON

Monday 22 April 1935

Gem / Regal
Station Road

"It was opened with a bold flourish on Easter Monday, 1935," recalled Dorothy Cleal in *Hertfordshire Countryside* (August 1998). "I remember the day, because our local shop displayed a poster advertising the event, and the accompanying picture was of a chick bursting out of an Easter Egg." There was a special matinée at 2.30pm on the day that the Gem Super Cinema opened and the first three-day programme consisted of *The Campbells are Coming* with Jack Hulbert supported by *Re-Union* with Lila Lee. The building was designed on modern lines by architect E.M. Allen-Hallatt for L.G. Attree, an electrician from Bishop's Stortford who operated the cinema and appointed E.J. 'Chips' Carpenter as the first manager.

The 607 seats were essentially on a single floor – there was only a step to separate the 'balcony' from the stalls. Prices of admission for adults ranged from sixpence to 2/- and there were two boxes at the rear costing 10/- each and seating up to five. There was parking space for 100 cars at the back and accommodation for bicycles. There was also a café. Early programming made a point of including one of the very popular Mickey Mouse cartoons in each show.

This is one of the clearest examples of a cinema that should never have been built. The low-cost conversion of an existing hall in the centre of Standon into a 250-seater might have made sense, but this was a cinema with over 600 seats to fill located amid green fields between Puckeridge and Standon, on the other side of the A120 from the village centre of the latter. It was 100 yards from the railway station and a quarter of a mile from the main Cambridge/London road. Giving it the old-fashioned name of the Gem was another indication that the owner was out of touch.

"The idea was, I gather, that people would come in from the surrounding villages and hamlets. But the little matter of transport had been overlooked," Dorothy Cleal wrote in her article. "There was a half-hearted attempt, after the first few unprofitable weeks, to lay on a bus touring the outlying villages to pick up customers, but the fare was a shilling, which, added to the cost of a seat, made it an expensive evening out for a family. The few people who had cars seemed to prefer the more sophisticated nightlife of Hertford, Ware or Stortford, where they could combine their cinema-going with other attractions. For those of us, the majority, who were carless, it was public transport or nothing. In my family's case, 'public transport' meant the train, this costing sixpence for an adult, threepence for children, return. The cheapest seats in the cinema were 6d and 3d also, right up the front, so that one's neck ached dreadfully.

"The train service was hardly geared to fit in with the cinema timetable, the consequence being that we never saw a whole film – not the main feature anyway... We alighted at Standon station (which made us think of 'Buggleskelly' in *Oh, Mr. Porter!*, so relaxed were its attendants). A short walk up the road then, and into the foyer of the Gem, savouring the atmosphere, the undefined glamour, and the smell – rose disinfectant mingling with, perhaps, the 'Evening in Paris' of the usherettes, who seemed to me like starlets themselves,

The Regal Standon in the 1950s. (The Cinema Museum.)

living lives of unimagined excitement and romance (though in fact depressingly underemployed).

"Inside, we would find ourselves halfway through the main feature, which would be going through its paces for an audience of perhaps ten. Then we would sit impatiently through the local advertisements, the only one I remember now said: 'Woman's Crowning Glory…Glorified!!' with suitable 'Before' and 'After' illustrations and the address of a little salon in the High Street. Then came the news, and the forthcoming attractions (which made one mentally swear to come next week, come what may). Then perhaps a cartoon and/or documentary about coal; then the 'B' picture, often featuring singing cowboys, as I recall, or the adventures of the Jones Family. And then, at last, with no more than half an hour left before our train was due, the main attraction, the end of which we had already seen. As the clock hands moved down towards 8.20, we had to edge our way towards the exit, with straining backwards glances, longing to see the exact point at which we had come in; but we never did, and with one last lingering look we had to tear ourselves away, out into pale reality and the gallop to catch the train – for it was the last one, and if we missed it we would have been faced with a five mile walk home. A taxi was undreamed of.

"In this piecemeal way we saw some of the great classics, and a good many of those best forgotten... We rarely saw anything that could be called a love story... 'Love' in the more adult sense was a closed book to us, and our mother was determined it should remain so... If despite her vigilance and the watchful eye of the Hays office, we found ourselves faced with a scene in which the characters started kissing with more enthusiasm than was seemly, we were instructed to shut our eyes. We didn't!"

In 1937 the Gem was taken over by Lou Morris, a prominent figure in film exhibition who also features in the history of Watford's cinemas. He evidently decided the cinema might work with a fresh start and it closed on 7 August with the promise of new carpets, sound equipment and electrical fittings when it re-opened. Lou Morris's usual architects, J. Owen Bond and Sons, drew up plans for the alterations. It was re-launched with the modern name of Regal on Thursday 2 September 1937, advertising itself as "now completely redecorated, re-seated and re-furnished... the COSIEST cinema in Herts" (the word "cosiest" was probably a sly dig at its rival, the Cosy at Buntingford). Seating seems to have increased to 644 (hardly cosy) and apparently there was a 10ft deep stage and two dressing rooms (although they might have existed since the first opening).

For four years during the war, the Regal was turned into a sugar store. It re-opened on Monday 3 February 1947 with a three-day run of *Theirs is the Glory*, a war documentary. The cinema was now operated by a small circuit, London & Provincial Cinemas, whose seventeen halls in 1947 also included the Cinema at Radlett and the Publix Stevenage. L & P found the going so tough by the late 1950s that the Regal was put up for sale, along with an adjacent house and the vacant land around. An attempt was made to improve business by closing on Wednesdays and Thursdays and by removing the front stalls (reducing seating to 385) for rock 'n' roll sessions on Wednesday evenings. Patronage declined to the extent that only one customer turned up for one show (which was cancelled) and a few weeks later the Regal was closed. The last programme was a two-day run of *Carry On Regardless* concluding on Saturday 30 September 1961. Miss Phyllis Parker, who had been the cinema's cashier throughout its life, recalled that the only time there had ever been a queue was on opening night.

In later years, the building was converted into the premises of the Willesden Transformer Company and the Cameron Instrument Company. The ground floor of the auditorium was levelled off and an upper floor inserted. Windows were punched into the walls and the front bricked in with an extension built on the side for the reception area and offices. It still seemed possible to make out where the name of Regal had appeared on the upper brickwork but that was the only indication of its past history as a picture house.

By 2002, the building had vanished to make way for new houses, seemingly those at the end of Orchard Drive. Only a Regal Close of other new houses nearby hints at the cinema of yesteryear but this is not where it stood.

STEVENAGE

Thursday 8 January 1914

Cinema / Publix

5 Bowling Green

The Stevenage Cinema with the War Memorial to left, circa 1920. (Stevenage Museum.)

Films had come earlier to Stevenage circa 1910 with Charles Thurston's touring shows, followed by the Castle Cinema in White Lion Meadow, New Road, which was a temporary structure dismantled after ten months in late February 1914, evidently knocked out by the arrival of the Cinema.

The conversion of a hall attached to a restaurant at the north end of old Stevenage, just off the High Street at the back of the triangular Bowling Green, the Cinema seated around 300, including a tiny balcony. It closed late 1916/early 1917, seemingly for lack of a projectionist (the First World War had claimed most male cinema staff). However, it re-opened on Monday 27 January 1919 after some alterations, and shows combined variety and pictures. Saturday children's matinées were held at 2pm.

The Cinema may have been briefly called the Tudor; it certainly changed its name to Publix in April 1935 and responded to the opening of the Astonia with larger advertisements and competitive slogans. (The name Publix may have been suggested by the American film company called Paramount Publix which became Paramount Pictures.)

In 1943 a Council inspection noted 218 stalls seats and 98 in the circle. In 1944 the Publix became part of the small London and Provincial circuit which also operated the cinemas at Radlett and Standon. Its small capacity left it at a disadvantage compared to the Astonia. Former patrons recall

wooden benches at the front even in the 1950s – and the sound of rats scurrying about. It had become a real dump.

Like other cinemas in its position, the Publix tried Continental films with adults-only X certificates and these, changed Mondays and Thursdays, formed the bulk of programming in its last days. Despite sensational advertising, many of the films had

A wider view of the Stevenage Cinema after it had become the Publix in the mid-1930s with a new, taller frontage. Notice restaurant sign to left.

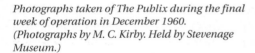

Photographs taken of The Publix during the final week of operation in December 1960.
(Photographs by M. C. Kirby. Held by Stevenage Museum.)

considerable artistic merit. Some improvements and redecoration took place but the building was in need of structural repairs. It closed on 31 December 1960 after a three-day run of the Italian X film *The Last Meeting* supported by *The House in the Woods*. Demolition took place in October 1965.

By 1985, the site was occupied by part of a short row of houses (numbers 5, 6 and 7 Bowling Green), although the former restaurant next door was still operating. In 2002, the restaurant has become a private house.

Saturday 20 April 1935

Astonia

Pound Avenue
(corner of Letchmore Road)

The Astonia Stevenage, just prior to closing. (Stevenage Museum.)

The Astonia was built for Noel A. Ayres (who later opened another cinema of the same name in Baldock) and it had 750 seats on one floor. The architect was H. W. J. Dutton of Knebworth. Why 'Astonia' rather than Astoria? Martin Ayres has explained: "When my parents were trying to think of a name, they had a party with several friends attending and the topic again came up as to what to call the new cinema. One bright person suggested that as my father's full name was Noel Aston Ayres the middle name be used, adding only the 'ia'. This was readily adopted by my parents."

The Astonia was a great improvement on the Publix and for many years enjoyed good support from the town. In the 1960s, even though the Publix had closed and the town's population had surged to 60,000, the Astonia fell prey to hooliganism and gained such a bad reputation that Martin Ayres, who had succeeded his father as director and part-owner, tried banning teenagers for a while. The Astonia had also slipped behind other towns in obtaining new films and seemed little better placed than its sister theatre in Baldock. The last straw came when the Rank Organisation announced plans for a new Odeon in 1968 in the centre of the New Town development area immediately to the south – with its better position and taking at least half the new films (probably the best half), the prospects for the Astonia looked grim. Martin Ayres decided to cater for better-behaved audiences with bingo and announced the change-over in September 1968. On Saturday 1 March 1969, after a seven-day run of the Steve McQueen/Faye Dunaway caper film, *The Thomas Crown Affair*, with supporting feature *Submarine X-1*, the Astonia's days as a cinema ended, even though no Odeon was built.

The Astonia Bingo and Social Club operated until 4 March 1982. Subsequently the building was leased to become the Stevenage Snooker club, painted beige with the old entrance blocked in under a larger brown canopy, reducing access to one door in the side. In 2002 the building remains in the same use as Riley's American Pool and Snooker. This is played on two floors with new low ceilings. There are no traces of the original cinema in the playing areas except possibly for some simple triangular decoration on the sloping beams on the upstairs side walls.

Sunday 18 November 1973

ABC / Cannon

The Forum, St George's Way

When the new town centre was planned, the Development Corporation was anxious to include a cinema and a site was originally allocated in 1960 at the end of Danestrete to the north of the northwest car park. The two major circuits, Odeon and ABC, indicated that they might

be interested when the population reached the 40–50,000 mark, which it did later in the 1960s. The Rank Organisation eventually decided to build a new Odeon as it had done at Hemel Hempstead and Harlow – it turned down a site to the west of the new shopping centre because of the noise from the adjacent bus station and took a smaller site originally earmarked for a hotel. The new Odeon was announced in July 1968 and preliminary work began in April 1969 on an 850-seat cinema to cost £150,000 which was expected

The ABC Stevenage in 1985. (Photograph by Allen Eyles.)

The upstairs landing at the ABC Stevenage at opening in 1973.

The two auditoria of the ABC Stevenage at opening in 1973.

to open in December. Then Rank considered putting in two auditoria instead of one and otherwise re-examined the project, concluding in April 1970 that, with rising building costs and declining attendances, a free-standing building was no longer economically feasible. Hopes were then pinned on a new cinema being built above shops or in association with other commercial development and this is what eventually happened when the rival ABC chain opened two cinemas over the Tesco supermarket. These were the first cinemas ever built and opened by this huge national circuit in Hertfordshire.

The cinemas had a ground-floor foyer with kiosk and paybox plus a staircase to a licensed bar on the first floor and to the two auditoria. ABC 1, with 340 seats, opened with *Jesus Christ Superstar* and ABC 2, with 182 seats, opened with the James Bond film *Live and Let Die.* (In November 1975, the Stevenage Leisure Centre on Lytton Way opened and its Gordon Craig Theatre also showed films as part of the activities.)

The ABC cinemas took the name Cannon with effect from Friday 13 February 1987 to reflect a change of ownership that had taken place some months before. A tiny weekly advertisement in the *Stevenage Express* hardly suggested any confidence in the drawing power of the twin cinema. In 1989 the Cannon was threatened by a redevelopment scheme by the landlords, Trafalgar House, which wanted to use the shell of the cinemas for retail units. The local authority requested Trafalgar House to find a new site for the cinemas.

As the Cannon 1 and 2, the cinemas survived this threat only to close on 7 April 1994 when it was stated they had been losing a considerable amount of money – which should not have been the case. The later multiplex has demonstrated the huge demand for cinema in the area although its arrival would have undoubtedly caused the twin cinema's demise.

Monday 8 July and Friday 12 July 1996

Cineworld The Movies / Cineworld

Stevenage Leisure Park, Six Hills Way

This multiplex was the first venture of a new British company, Cine-UK, which had raised capital in 1995 to bid for the UK's Cannon-MGM circuit. When this was acquired by Virgin, Cine-UK decided to redeploy the money to establish a series of multiplexes in new leisure developments, concentrating on the less competitive markets and less expensive sites. TBI's leisure park scheme at Stevenage was handily close to the A1 motorway (and even closer to the railway station) but any cinema development had to compete with UCI's established multiplex over the motorway at Hatfield's Galleria. It became the site of Cine-UK's first Cineworld The Movies with twelve screens seating a total of 2,167. This remained Cine-UK's sole operating cinema for five months until a second Cineworld opened at Wakefield, followed by a third at Feltham a year and a day after Stevenage made its bow. Cine-UK's American chief executive, Steve Wiener, formerly with Warner Bros Theatres, noted that rival companies were not impressed by its slow start. "Basically, they did not take us seriously," he recalled in the film trade paper, *Screen International* (20 November 1998). "They thought we'd build one cinema and that would be the end of it. And I have to say, when we opened our first cinema, the way it traded they might have been right. We opened Stevenage probably

The spacious foyer of the Cineworld Stevenage in a 1996 photograph (courtesy of Cine-UK). Baskin Robbins has since replaced Haagens Daz at the ice cream counter while the café area with chairs at back right has become a games station but will form the entrance for the four additional cinemas that are expected to open at the end of 2002. The Cineworld's exterior is shown on the front cover.

four months before the rest of the leisure park was finished so it was just us and McDonald's, and we were starving initially. But, as the leisure park got finished and stopped being a construction zone, it started improving."

The cinema is centrally placed at the back of the site with extensive areas for parking in front. It has a large peaked glass tower and a vast foyer with a ceiling that slopes towards the back and has a mirrored central section. Open to the roof and crossed by ventilation ducts, the upper area is painted black to be as inconspicuous as possible with strong down lights suspended. Above the concessions counter at the back of a foyer are machines which can be seen freshly popping the popcorn (which is then bagged and kept warm). The various screens are accessed from a corridor at the back right of the foyer which has a T junction leading to further screens at the end. As at Cineworld Bishop's Stortford, roped-off queueing areas are set up to hold patrons so that they can enter an auditorium more quickly when there are busy performances. One long projection room serves all the auditoria.

The individual seating figures for the twelve screens are: 357, 289, 175, 148, 88, 99, 137, 112, 168, 135, 173, and 286. The largest auditoria have stepped or stadium seating. (The 2,167 seats add up to the largest number in any cinema ever operated in Hertfordshire although these are spread over twelve auditoria and total only a few more the single auditoria of two of Watford's former cinemas.)

The cinema had a champagne launch on Monday 8 July 1996 when celebrity guests Bob Monkhouse and Mystic Meg cut a reel of film in the presence of the Mayor and Mayoress of Stevenage. The opening week's attractions included *Mission Impossible* (on two screens), *The Cable Guy* (on two screens), *The Rock, Moonlight and Valentino, Sense And Sensibility, Kingpin, Empire Records, Up Close and Personal* and *Down Periscope*. There was a one-day (Thursday) revival of *Schindler's List* and special previews *of The Hunchback of Notre Dame* on the Saturday and Sunday. Children's Saturday morning shows began with *Babe* at 10am. Late night shows played on all screens on Fridays and Saturdays, commencing between 10.40pm and 00.20am

A clear demonstration of Cineworld's success at Stevenage is that four additional screens are due to open around Christmas 2002. Expected to seat 176, 196, 231 and 246 respectively, these occupy part of a failed bingo club next door. How nice, for once, to see films replace bingo! Total seating capacity will rise to just over 3,000. The new cinemas will be reached from the back left of the foyer currently occupied by a games centre which will be moved elsewhere.

TRING

Saturday 23 November 1912

Gem
High Street

The Unity Hall was above the Tring Co-operative Society's shop; it held 300 people and with a 19ft deep stage was often used for plays. Then a group called the Enterprise Cinema Syndicate made considerable alterations and turned it into the Gem Picture Hall. P. J. Darvell, who was the licensee in 1916, decided to replace it with a purpose-built Gem and it closed when his new cinema was ready to open. In 1985 the premises were banqueting rooms.

Saturday 29 July 1916

Empire Picture Theatre / Gaiety
Akeman Street

The first Gem was doing so well that a certain William Charles Wilson had plans drawn up by architect Fred Taylor of Aylesbury for a purpose-built cinema to seat 250 on a raked stalls floor and 64 in a small balcony. A race developed to open before the new Gem and this was the winner by a few days. A then local resident, Mr A. Williams, much later recalled that the projector was powered by a gas engine and on the opening night the film kept fading on the screen as the belt drive was slipping off the dynamo. The Empire survived these teething problems and (like Mr Wilson's Palace at Chesham) went on to become, for a while, the only cinema in town.

Front elevation of the Empire Tring as built.

In 1932 the name was changed to the Gaiety and later proprietors were A. C. Powell and Basil Green. When the new Regal opened in 1936 it had a severe effect and the Gaiety closed soon after war broke out in 1939. In 1985 it had been adapted into the engineering works of William Batey with a new extension added to the top of the building.

Tuesday 1 August 1916

Gem

Western Road

The purpose-built premises of the new Gem were almost opposite the end of Henry Street. Local architect A. C. Saunders' plans allowed for 387 seats. Proprietor P.J. Darvell was horrified by the construction of the rival Empire, declaring that a town of

4,481 people was not large enough for two picture houses. He was right – and the Gem lasted only until the early 1920s. It was later demolished. In 1985 its site was occupied by United Dairies.

Thursday 10 September 1936

Regal

Western Road

The Regal was one of a number of cinemas of the same name, all built to a very similar design (architect: Harold S. Scott) with wide, plain brick frontages and attractive single-floor auditoria behind. Other such Regals were at Atherstone, Cirencester, Dursley, Hayling Island, Odiham and Trowbridge, but the Tring Regal, seating only 514, was one of the smallest. It was promoted by a company of Birmingham wine merchants and opened with *Come out of the Pantry* (starring Jack Buchanan and Fay Wray) supported by shorts and a newsreel.

It did superb business during the war, thanks to the thousands of evacuated children and the American forces stationed at Marsworth. It became part of the Mayfair circuit when that was formed in the early 1940s and passed to the large ABC circuit along with all the other Mayfair cinemas around 1943, making it the first ABC outlet in Hertfordshire. The Regal was not, however, regarded with any great pride by its new owners. Barring took away the best films until three weeks after they had played Aylesbury and Hemel Hempstead and by 1958 it was a long-standing loss-maker, overdue for closure, when all matinées had been cut (it opened daily around 4.30pm).

The Regal closed at very short notice on Saturday 15 February 1958 after concluding a three-day run of *Gunfight at the OK Corral*

The Regal Tring, circa 1946.

WALTHAM CROSS

Monday 20 October 1913
Electric Palace / Palace / Regent
77 High Street

supported by *At the Stroke of Nine*. The high rate of Entertainments Tax was blamed. This did not deter an independent operator from taking a lease and re-opening the cinema on 6 April 1958 but his efforts were in vain and the Regal was forced to close again on 19 March 1960. ABC disposed of the property on 20 September 1961.

The Regal came to life once more on 20 November 1965 as the Masque Theatre with a brand-new musical production of *Heidi* but its career as a live theatre terminated after a few shows and the scenery of the last production was left in situ. Seventeen different planning applications had been made for the site before the building was demolished in late 1978/early 1979 – permissions had sometimes been granted but not put into effect. In the end, ten flats were built on the site and given the name of Regal Court.

Local showman Captain Cecil Clayton brought films to the area by hiring Trinity Hall in Marsh Lane, putting up a screen and seating audiences on hard wooden benches. His company, Clayton Bros, then erected the Electric Palace with 600 seats on a sloping floor and a projection box above the entrance. Seats at 6d and 9d were 'tip-ups' upholstered in plush but only some of those at 3d were padded. As usual with early cinemas, gas provided the heating while electricity (from a 16 horsepower engine) provided the lighting and power for the projection equipment. The first show was headed by *Mystery of the Great Diamond*, while from Thursday the top attraction was *The Accusing Hand*. Children's shows were held on Saturdays at 2.30pm.

Captain V. A. Haskett-Smith took over the Palace in the mid-1920s and sold it to the Shipman & King circuit in 1931. They closed it on 20 June 1931 after a week of 'Old Favourites' concluding with *The Hollywood Revue*. When it re-opened, renamed the Regent, on Monday 5 October, it had been redecorated, entirely re-seated and had new heating, ventilation and sound equipment as well as a new entrance to the side of the auditorium. It now seated 700 and offered a car park for 100 cars. The architects for the conversion were Howis and Belcham.

In the mid-1930s S & K was anxious to enlarge the Regent to meet the demand for seats but, being thwarted in attempts to

*The Palace Waltham Cross on re-opening as the
Regent in October 1931.*

acquire enough adjacent land, built a
second cinema, the Embassy, nearly opposite. This was by far the better of the two
halls but the Regent continued until 1972
when EMI (which now owned S & K)
decided to concentrate film business on the
Embassy, converting it to three screens. The
Regent became the sole cinema in town for
three months while the Embassy was subdivided. Its last new attraction was the Burt
Reynolds drama *Deliverance* which played
from Sunday 29 October for seven days, but
the final screen presentation was a one-day
revival of *The Devil Rides Out* and *The Lost
Continent* on Sunday 5 November. (The

Embassy re-opened the next day.) Advertising said that the Regent "closes for alterations". The alterations that took place were
for Mecca bingo from 1973, for which purpose the auditorium was well maintained
with its decorative bands across the low ceiling still intact, ending in cherubs on the side
walls. But bingo ceased in 1986 and the
Regent's auditorium was demolished during
the following year. The cinema entrance
alongside survived, but completely transformed, being the premises of health club
Eternal Youth in 2002. The original rendering has vanished, exposing brickwork. A
new building has appeared alongside, occu-
pying the front part of the auditorium.
Behind this, in place of the remainder of the
auditorium, is a car park and adjacent flats.

Thursday 18 November 1937

Embassy / Cannon

High Street

The Embassy opened with Robert Taylor
and Barbara Stanwyck in *His Affair* supported by Don Ameche in *Fifty Roads to
Town*. Designed by Howis and Belcham with
interior decoration by Mollo and Egan, it
was one of several extremely attractive cinemas built for the Shipman & King circuit in
the mid to late 1930s. Internally, it was very
similar to the Embassys at Chesham and
Esher, both opened earlier in 1937 and decorated by Mollo and Egan. Along with the
same decorator's Odeon North Watford, it
had the finest 1930s auditorium of any
cinema in Hertfordshire. There were approximately 1,700 seats.

The less spectacular but well-handled
frontage, in red brick with faience trim-
mings, was set back from the main road and
looked at its most attractive when decora-

The Embassy Waltham Cross in 1937.

tive neon was switched on at night. The foyer had a low ceiling with round art deco light fittings set into recesses, boldly striped rubber flooring – and a back wall with box-office windows, wood panelling with chrome trim and an illuminated high-level mural showing vividly coloured tropical foliage designed by Eugene Mollo. (A similar decorative band and ceiling treatment were seen in Mollo and Egan's work at the Gaumont Rose Hill, Surrey, opened six months earlier.) There was a café over the entrance with more panels of colourful foliage on the side walls.

The most striking feature of the auditorium was the repetitive squares of decorative grillework on the splay walls to each side of the proscenium arch, each square front lit by a concealed light in the centre. Thirty-five squares were arranged on each side in rows of seven across by five down, with the top row extending across the top of the proscenium arch to link the two sides. (There was no such link in the otherwise very similar decorative schemes at Chesham and Esher.) In addition, a long recess in the ceiling, lit by concealed lighting, directed the eye towards the screen area. The Embassy had a Christie organ taken from the Court Berkhamsted with a French trumpet added. The walls were originally silver-grey and the seats red and grey. There was a proper stage with five dressing rooms.

The Granada circuit made tentative plans to open a rival cinema in Waltham Cross, revealed in a surviving letter written in June 1939 by architects Nicholas and

The Embassy Waltham Cross in 1937. Notice decorative frieze by Eugene Mollo above paybox.

The café-restaurant at the Embassy Waltham Cross in 1937. The striking decoration of the upper far wall is very similar to that which Eugene Mollo supplied to the circle foyer of the Odeon North Watford.

Dixon-Spain seeking payment for their work to date. The increasing threat of war – and, perhaps, second thoughts – made Granada respond that the scheme was "unlikely to move" and S & K retained a local monopoly on screen entertainment.

The Embassy was the first S & K site to install a CinemaScope screen in 1954. It was also the first to be subdivided into three smaller cinemas, closing for reconstruction on Saturday 5 August 1972 after a week's run of *Mutiny on the Buses*. An inevitable but regrettable consequence of the £65,000 conversion was the loss of the side wall decor of the auditorium, the proscenium arch (hidden from view) and the organ (which departed to a private residence). (It is still possible to enjoy the very similar decorative scheme at Esher where the listed Embassy has become the Odeon, the auditorium more sensitively adapted to fit two extra cinemas on the stalls floor.)

Re-opening took place on Monday 6 November 1972. Embassy 1 began with *The Godfather* and seated 460 in the old circle area with a new screen in front, using the original projection box. Embassy 2 with 284

seats, which opened with *Tower of Evil* plus *Demons of the Mind*, and Embassy 3 with 103 seats, which opened with *What's Up Doc?*, were positioned to each side of a dividing wall down the former stalls with new screens and proscenium openings.

The tripled Embassy proved such a success that, from 12 March 1981, the former café area became a fourth cinema, seating 83 and using video. When video proved unsatisfactory, conventional 35mm projection was squeezed into the limited space and became functional from 7 March 1985. Though it has lost its former glory inside, the Embassy retained its original exterior neon display in the mid-1980s, creating a striking impression in red and blue after dark. By this time it had been taken over by EMI along with other surviving S & K theatres.

The cinema suffered from the absence of other entertainment facilities to bring the area to life in the evenings. It was further isolated when only buses, not cars, were allowed to drive past the entrance. And then there was vandalism which included an attempt to set the rear of the building on fire and damage to the wiring of

the neon on front which it was decided not to repair.

The splendid interior of the Embassy Waltham Cross in 1937 with the organ console raised to full view.

Many months after EMI sold both its ABC and S & K chains to the foreign Cannon group, the cinema took the cumbersome name of its new owners from Friday 10 April 1987. It closed on Thursday 16 September 1993 because of declining audiences. Most of its former patrons had defected to the UCI multiplex at Hatfield, a short distance away on the M1. A bargain basement price of £2.50 merely emphasised that this was no longer the place to be. The last pictures shown were *Sliver, Jurassic Park, Made in America* and *Hot Shots Part Deux*.

In 1994 the building was purchased by the Jasmine bingo chain which re-opened it in early 1996. This followed the removal of all the subdivision to return to a single auditorium, but what remained of the original side wall decoration was scrapped, along

with the original proscenium arch, to create a very plain interior. Subsequent bingo operators have been Zetters and Riva but it was part of the Gala chain in 2002.

Externally, there is a much narrower entrance with new tiling to each side that matches in colour but clashes in size with the original tilework above and to each side. A ponderous stepped canopy is painted blue. The Gala name sign is mounted on a blue background that blots out the windows above the canopy. The tall slit windows to each side have been covered up by vertical yellow strips. There is a desultory use of red neon. The old Embassy name survives in raised tilework high on the front elevation.

The glorious cinema foyer of 1937 has

totally gone, the space reduced in size with a false ceiling. The café area on the first floor has given way to partitions and offices. The auditorium is brightly decorated but the proscenium area has given way to seating at an upper level, extending back along each side wall to the balcony front, and to a café at the back of the stage. All that remains of the original decoration is the ceiling recess (no longer lit up from within) and some decorative plasterwork around the edge of the raised central ceiling area at the back of the balcony.

WARE

Tuesday 26 December 1911

Ware Picture Hall / Ware Cinema / Astoria
Amwell End

Ware's first and only purpose-built cinema opened on Boxing Day 1911 instead of the previous Thursday as originally announced. It had been built in five weeks for William Skipp on a prominent site between the railway station and the main thoroughfare. The frontage was in red brick and there were 400 seats in the hall which was heated by four gas radiators. A 10 horsepower gas engine provided light for the auditorium and power for the single hand-cranked projector. Free afternoon teas were served at the Thursday matinée. Film of local events was sometimes shown, as when footage of steeplechases on Saturday 12 April 1913 was screened throughout the following week. Before the Picture Hall opened, moving pictures had been shown at the Town Hall Assembly Rooms, and shows apparently continued there for a few years in competition with the new cinema. The Drill Hall opposite the new cinema was also licensed for films in 1913 and had occasional shows.

In 1925 the Picture Hall gained new owners who installed two new projectors and renamed it the Ware Cinema. In the 1930s the Cinema became old-fashioned compared with its more modern rivals at Hertford and Hoddesdon and it was taken over late in the decade by a W. H. Reynolds who planned major alterations. These were probably a response to plans that were advanced in November 1938 by architect

The Astoria at Ware, still called Cinema as well, circa 1964.

J. E. Farrell on behalf of the owners of the Welwyn Pavilion to build a new 862-seat Pavilion cinema in Ware. The Pavilion was, of course, never built – perhaps because of the war, perhaps because of the proposed upgrading of the Cinema.

But it was not until 1948 that the Cinema was thoroughly modernised. By this time Mr Reynolds had died and Charles Ballands was in charge. He had begun here as a re-wind boy at the age of thirteen and progressed to chief operator and then manager before becoming part-owner. New fire regulations necessitated major alterations to the tiny projection room (10ft x 8ft) which was situated in the vestibule. It was decided to drastically improve not only the operating box but the entire building. Plans were drawn up by Hertford architect J. B. Healing and as much work as possible was done without closing – during one week audiences watched films under a roof that was being slowly raised by 5ft 6ins. The Cinema then shut for three weeks after a Sunday revival programme of *Bluebeard* plus *China's Little*

Devils on 3 October. The auditorium was literally turned round to take advantage of 27ft of available space at the rear of the building which was used to extend outwards and add another ninety seats with spacious new pro-

The foyer of the Astoria Ware, circa 1970. (Photograph by Kevin S. Wheelan.)

In this view to the rear of the Astoria Ware, note the barrier between the front seats and the rear. (Photograph by Kevin S. Wheelan.)

jection facilities built over them. The screen was now placed in a new proscenium arch at the front end of the building and the slope of the auditorium floor was reversed. There were 240 new seats along with 190 reconditioned ones and a barrier was built across the auditorium to separate the more expensive seats from the front rows – a passage along the side of the auditorium provided separate access to the rear section. The foyer was rebuilt at a lower level that eliminated the old entrance steps and internally the cinema had been utterly transformed.

It was re-named the Astoria for its gala re-opening on Saturday 23 October 1948 which began a special five-day run of the film *London Belongs to Me*. On the Saturday, film stars Jimmy Hanley and his wife, Dinah Sheridan, made personal appearances. Normally, the cinema played films weeks after Hertford and Hoddesdon but this once it had the jump on the opposition as *London Belongs to Me* opened concurrently on the following Monday at the County Hertford but not in Hoddesdon until the day after its run in Ware. But when a "giant wide screen" was introduced on Monday 29 November

1954 the first feature shown on it was *House of Wax* which had played at the Castle Hertford more than three months earlier.

The only new first-run films the Astoria could obtain were Continental ones and three-day (Monday to Wednesday) bookings of foreign double bills became a monthly event in 1954. Late in the 1950s Charles Ballands tried to boost attendances with live musical interludes and concerts on the tiny stage that featured then little known artists such as Cliff Richard, but the best solution proved to be part-time bingo.

The Astoria became the first cinema in Hertfordshire to succumb to bingo and almost the only one not to eventually surrender to it full-time. This was because Charles Ballands remained a cinema enthusiast at heart and used bingo to subsidise the film side. He publicised his film programmes at bingo sessions and even showed trailers.

Bingo first came in on Wednesdays and on Sunday afternoons from 9 October 1963. It also took over on Fridays from 10 April 1964. But that was it – five nights were left for films! This was very much a family business with Charles' wife looking after the paybox and kiosk side of the operation. They were now sole joint owners. First, Mrs Ballands died and then Charles followed her, aged 60, on 14 April 1975. The business was carried on by his two married daughters and a family friend, Olive Cowell, in the hope of selling it as a going concern. (These biographical details come from notes by Kevin S. Wheelan in the *Cinema Theatre Association Bulletin*, July 1979.)

Such a sale did not prove possible and the Astoria closed on Saturday 31 March 1979 after a five-day run of the Burt Reynolds film *Hooper* interspersed with two final nights of bingo. The two Kalee 8 projectors with modifications had been in service

The auditorium of the Astoria Ware, circa 1970. The exits seem to have prevented a wider proscenium opening and the CinemaScope screen must have been minute. The floral panels over the right exit are partly covered by dark curtains hiding a bingo score board. (Photograph by Kevin S. Wheelan.)

since 1928. One of them was restored by former chief projectionist Ashford Gibson, working with the Projected Picture Trust, and saved for display in a local museum.

By 1985 the building had become the Beckets Walk arcade of fifteen small shopping units on the ground floor (the steps up the central passageway are a reminder of the upward incline of the cinema floor). The frontage was much altered but a nightclub on the upper floor (earlier called Beckets, but renamed Club Nautica in 2002) at least maintains the entertainment use of the building.

WATFORD

Saturday 2 October 1909

Kinetic Picture Palace / Electric Picture Palace

Corn Exchange, Market Place

Moving pictures reached Watford as early as Monday 8 March 1897 when films from pioneer R.W. Paul were part of Madame Newsome's Grand Circus presentation at the Clarendon Hall. Travelling companies set up their screens in Watford regularly – notably William F. Jury's Imperial Bioscope Company which came each year from 1905 to 1909.

It was evident that Watford could support a full-time cinema. Corn exchanges provided a large indoor space that could be used for showing films, and arrangements were made to rent the one in Watford, except on Tuesdays when it was needed for its marketing function. Two hours of shorts were shown afternoon and evening. Business prospered and a balcony incorporating a new projection box was added at the High Street end of the 60ft by 30ft auditorium. Originally called the Kinetic Picture Palace, it was called the Electric Picture Palace in January 1914 and seems to have petered out in the autumn of that year.

Thursday 16 December 1909

Conservative Club Annexe

Clarendon Road
(corner with High Street)

Others also saw the potential for showing films in Watford. The new Palace Theatre in Clarendon Road screened films in music hall programmes and even became primarily a cinema from 27 June to 30 July 1910. Local photographer and film booking agent F. Downer formed a company, Bipics Ltd, to establish a cinema in another suitable large space, the Conservative Club Annexe. It seems to have faded out by May 1910 but, as there was a raked or stepped floor to provide a clearer view of the screen from all the seats, it was an attempt to provide a proper cinema.

Friday 19 May 1911

Cinema Palace

134 High Street

This was a more elaborate attempt to establish a cinema in Watford. The

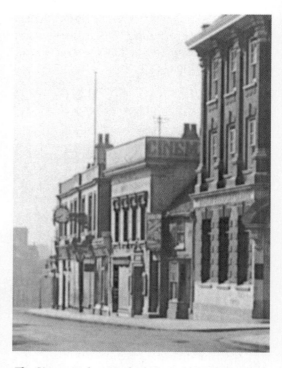

The Cinema Palace Watford, circa 1912. The building on the corner stands relatively unaltered and was unoccupied in March 2002 but the short-lived Cinema Palace next door is no longer evident in any way. (Watford Libraries.)

premises formerly occupied by solicitors William Thomas Boydell were converted into a 500-seat cinema on one floor for Counties Electric Theatres Ltd. The architect was E. H. C. Inskip (who also worked on alterations to the Picturedrome Hitchin). There were marble steps, potted palms, plush tip-up seats, and a small orchestra to accompany the silent films. Highlights of the opening programme were a coloured "art drama" *The Easter Egg* and film of the unveiling of the Victoria Memorial.

Despite its central position, the Cinema Palace failed to obtain the best films and had a succession of tenants. It seems to have been closed for almost all of 1914, reopened at the end of the year, and shut down permanently about April 1915.

The building, near the corner with King Street, later became the ABC tearooms and Williams' furniture store. The site is now occupied by Taylor's Café-Bar with no trace of the old frontage or interior.

Tuesday 1 October 1912

Electric Coliseum / Coliseum / Plaza

149 St Albans Road (corner of Bedford Street)

Coliseum Watford circa 1912. (Courtesy of Tony Moss.)

This 650-seat cinema was out of the town centre, just to the north of the railway tracks, on the main road going north. It catered for the people in the rows of terraced houses all around this part of Watford. The wall at the screen end of the auditorium extended along narrow Bedford Street and the original entrance was rather curiously placed on the side wall along the main St Albans Road nearer the front than the back of the hall. Doors on each side of the narrow open entrance led to different sections of seating. The architect was Henry F. Mence who had designed the Chequers cinema at St Albans for the same proprietors.

The first big attraction was *The Black Panther*. Films were accompanied on an Ascherberg piano or (on special occasions) by a "sweet toned pipe organ". There were matinées on Tuesday, Wednesday and Saturday and a special children's programme on Saturday between 1 lam and 1pm.

The Electric Coliseum proved especially popular with local troops during World War I. After the war, the adjacent property at the projection end was acquired and demolished so that the cinema could be enlarged to around 900 seats and a new entrance created at the back corner. The old entrance on the side was removed with only an exit

being provided in its place. The architects were Mence and Finn of St Albans.

It became one of the last Watford cinemas to surrender to the talkies. When sound was installed, the cinema was further extended at the back to create a larger foyer and it re-opened on 25 June 1930, advertising itself as the New Coliseum, seating around 1,000 on one floor, with Italian views painted on the side walls.

Further improvements took place when it closed on Thursday 3 December 1936 and a strikingly modern curving frontage was added to the back of the auditorium at the corner of St Albans Road with Railway Cottages. The cinema re-opened on 21 December under the control of Larry Webb (whose father, Captain F. A. Webb, ran the Chequers St Albans) and, taking advantage of the fact that the opulent Plaza in Watford has just been re-named Odeon, rather impudently styled itself "The New Plaza" for a while in advertising and "Plaza" on the front of the building in a vertical sign placed on the corner tower. The upper area of the corner was clad in light vitrolite while the base, below a new canopy, was in black vitrolite crossed by broad horizontal green bands.

From the late 1930s to December 1952, the Plaza was part of Southan Morris's substantial circuit of SM Super Cinemas (known as SM Associated Cinemas from 1948) but very secondary to its other Watford holding, the Regal. It then passed to smaller groups and played very weak programmes, for three days at most. It now seated 840 and had become the least of Watford's cinemas.

Rather than spend money to re-equip itself for the new wide screen era, the Plaza closed a week before CinemaScope arrived in Watford. Its final programme was *Bomba and the Jungle Girl* plus *Wild Stallion*, shown from 4.30pm for three days to Saturday 31 July 1954. This was the second post-war cinema closure in Hertfordshire. Demolition took place in 1957 and the site is occupied in 2002 by the Central Tyre service centre for motorists.

Thursday 6 November 1913

Empire / ABC / Cannon / ABC

Merton Road
(corner of Victoria Passage)

The Empire was designed by local architect William Grace and opened with just under 800 seats including a small balcony. It had an exclusive presentation of *Heroes of the Mine* on its aluminium screen (it was only later when speakers were placed behind that a lighter, perforated screen became essential). A small orchestra was a regular feature from mid-January 1914 (clearly, a pianist or trio of musicians had been used before this). In mid-March 1914, it was leased by a London concern, Majestic Theatres, but it closed soon after, to be re-opened in November by its original proprietors. From the first, the Empire had to fight its poor location on the edge of the town centre (ironically, this proved to be the key to its longevity as its site has not been coveted by developers). "Top of Market Street" was its address in 1927 press advertising, although you had to be right at the end to see it. At this time it called itself "The Cosiest Cinema in Watford", although a mite large for such a claim.

When talkies arrived, the Empire initially made a point of its fidelity to silent films, then changed tack, closing on 9 August 1930 and re-opening a few weeks later on 1 September with a modern sound system to show a film called *Charming Sinners*. As other new cinemas opened up in the centre of town, the Empire's competitive position worsened. Who would then have prophesied that it would outlast all its rivals of the time?

The Empire made do with what it could get. In 1945/6 it was "Watford's repertory cinema". Re-issues, foreign films, and second or third runs of recent hits formed the bulk of its programming into the 1970s. Occasionally it would gain a specialised film like *The Royal Ballet* (played for a season in June 1960) which did not appeal to the Odeon, Gaumont, Essoldo or Carlton.

If it had been a circuit-owned house, it might have gained better films. It was modernised in 1952 and again in 1965 when the frontage and auditorium were drastically altered, removing or concealing all the 1913 detail, so it obviously managed to pay its way. Seating came down to a total of 538. Then in 1973, Vicary Leisure (the owners since 1949) agreed to lease it to Bass Charrington for conversion into a pub and discothèque. Fortunately, all the necessary permissions were not forthcoming and the Empire continued as a cinema.

On 19 December 1976, the cinema was taken over by the S & K circuit (which was now owned by the major EMI company) and immediately its programming improved. The week before it had shown *Clockwork Nympho* plus *Sextet*; now it had a first run of *The Marathon Man*.

It was planned to twin the Empire but there was a booking dispute with the Rank Organisation whose Odeon and Carlton cinemas had been accustomed to first pick of all the new releases. EMI had taken over the major ABC circuit in February 1969 and demanded that the films booked to the ABC circuit should open in Watford at the Empire. After business on 31 May 1980, conversion to a twin began and Rank responded by closing the Carlton before the Empire reopened.

The Empire actually increased its seating in the twinning process. There had been 396 seats in the stalls and 142 in the balcony. It re-opened on Thursday 21 August 1980 with 363 seats in Empire 1 (the old stalls) and 204 seats in Empire 2 (the balcony extended forward) – a total of 567. *Fame* and *Airplane* were the attractions.

When EMI amalgamated its S & K and ABC circuits, the former's sites were allowed to retain their original names – with the exception of Watford. It is indicative of the importance EMI attached to their Watford outlet that, when it became the only cinema in the town (after the 1983 closure of the more central three-screen Odeon), it was re-branded ABC 1 and 2 from Friday 24 May 1985 following redecoration and the installation of Dolby sound in the larger auditorium.

ABC developed plans for a new multiplex in the Watford area but these were dropped by the Cannon company after it took over the ABC circuit in August 1986. A new vertical sign at the left end of the building went up and the cinema became the Cannon from Friday 12 December 1986.

The Empire Watford circa 1912. (Courtesy of Noreen Foskett.)

The Empire Watford circa 1977. (Photograph by Keith Skone.)

As the Cannon, it celebrated its eightieth birthday in 1993 with a different film on each day of the week. From January 1996, after the Cannon circuit had been taken over by Virgin and the older properties acquired by a new ABC company, it attempted to co-exist with the newly opened Warner multiplex at Woodside

Leisure Park. At more than two miles apart, both cinemas should have been able to survive. As an incentive, prices at the Cannon were cut so that adults paid £3 (compared with £4.30 at the Warner) and children were admitted for £2 (£3 at the Warner). This did, however, smack of desperation and its regular advertisement in the local paper was minute and hard to find as it was shunted around the page. There was sufficient confidence to change the cinema's name to ABC with effect from Friday 21 June but only three months later, on 19 September, it closed with *Independence Day* and *Diabolique* as its final attractions. It had remained open all day to the end rather than cutting matinées. Attendances during 1996 in competition with the multiplex were said to have fallen to half the level of the year before.

Although it had been completely altered over the years, its run of nearly eighty-three years as a cinema sets a record that no other Hertfordshire cinema has matched. In early 2002, it had become the Al Zahra Centre, divided into two floors of offices and rooms with windows inserted into the side wall along Victoria Passage. The old car park behind the cinema (with only thirty-five parking spaces) remains in use. A flat-floored upper room near the front of the building, reached by the stairs to the former balcony, is used for religious meetings. The frontage is boarded up but the 'light box' that announced the current film titles has been removed along with the covering of modern tiles at the top of the two columns supporting the entrance arch. This has exposed some of the original decorative detail, including the capitals of the columns, suggesting the entrance may regain some of its old appearance.

Wednesday 17 December 1913

Central Hall / Regal / Essoldo

19-21 King Street (corner of Granville Road)

Watford's first large cinema was built to plans of Norfolk and Prior which show seating for 748 in the stalls and 330 in the balcony. In fact, it was so large it was not quite full on the opening night when an audience that included the Earl of Clarendon, Lord and Lady Hyde, and Mr Moss, "the leading comedian with the Hepworth [Film] Company", laughed at the humour of *A Regiment for Two* and saw, among other items, "interest films" on performing the tango and waltz and on the cocoa industry. As normally happened, the first night was in aid of charity.

The Central Hall was open from 2.30pm daily except Sundays. Balcony seats were 6d, 9d and 1/-; the "area" [stalls] was 3d and 6d. Children, of course, had reduced prices. Despite its size, the cinema originally managed with only a pianist, aided by a cellist from 5pm, rather than an orchestra. Special films of children's stories were included at matinées in 1915. In the same year producer/performer Harry Hemsley appeared with his own comedy film and spoke the lines using different voices for the various characters in an attempt to make the silent screen 'speak' (Hemsley later became a well-known radio performer).

In the later 1920s the Central Hall was operated by D and M Cinemas. The company went into voluntary liquidation in the summer of 1929, owing £13,206 to film distributors and other creditors who were likely to realise less than a shilling in the pound. The Central Hall had become old-fashioned

Central Hall Watford, circa 1926.

installation of sound equipment and new seats totalling 1,263.

In 1932 the Regal became one of the Bernstein Theatres (the company which created the Granada circuit) and the Regal "Where Everybody Goes" (as the advertising optimistically put it) closed on Monday 21 November 1932 for inside reconstruction and redecoration to plans of architect George Coles and Theodore Komisarjevsky, the interior designer of Granada cinemas. Work was carried out around the clock and the Regal re-opened on Boxing Day with the highly popular British film, *Rome Express*, "direct from the Tivoli [Strand]". Regrettably, the new decor was rather plain and far from the opulent style of the celebrated Granadas. There were now 1,286 seats. After all this investment, Granada rather oddly lost interest in the property and it passed to a London company called Courtwood Cinemas.* Further improvements designed by George Coles were made in 1935 – mainly the modern frontage with a central tower that survives, much modified, to this day.

From the war years, the Regal was part of the large SM Super Cinemas circuit of Southan Morris and it profited greatly by playing the weekly ABC circuit release in the absence of an ABC theatre in the town. It also took the plunge into CinemaScope at an early date: a new 40 feet long/17 feet high screen was installed with speakers for four-track magnetic stereophonic sound. It was the only cinema in the area to install stereo

The Essoldo Watford. (The Cinema Museum.)

The auditorium of the former Essoldo Watford as a bingo hall on 2 June 1983. (Photograph by Allen Eyles.)

---

* According to Richard Gray's article on the architect David E. Nye in *Picture House* (no. 23, Summer 1997, pp. 52 and 54), Granada planned a return to Watford in 1948 when he was engaged to design a new cinema for a site in the town. I have come across no other record of this scheme (despite extensive research for a book on the history of Granada cinemas) and it may have been purely speculative and never submitted for planning approval.

and was poorly ventilated; it suffered badly in comparison with the new Plaza. Mortimer Dent's Standard Cinema Properties took over the lease and it re-opened as the Regal on 30 September 1929 after the at this time. The CinemaScope screen and surround sound were first used for a two-week run of the initial CinemaScope feature release, *The Robe,* from 9 August 1954.

The Newcastle-based Essoldo group took over the SM chain from 26 August 1954 but did not change the Regal's name until the week of 9 July 1956 when a 25 feet high vertical neon sign reading 'Essoldo' was erected. Now showing the pick of ABC and independently released Fox CinemaScope films with extended runs of films like *The King and I* and *The Ten Commandments*, the Essoldo could not fail to prosper for the rest of the 1950s. In the 1960s it seemed safe enough with the ABC release and extended runs of films like *Ben-Hur*, but it closed after a one-day booking on Sunday 17 November 1968 of *Castle of Terror* plus *I Married a Werewolf.* The last proper programme was *Hot Millions* supported by *The Funniest Man in the World* which had played from Sunday 10 November for seven days. Essoldo had decided to go after the richer pickings promised by bingo. In later years the building was operated for the same purpose by Ladbroke's, then by Top Rank, and under the latter's ownership it has been renamed Mecca, continuing in business in early 2002 (although closed on Wednesdays).

Saturday 12 February 1921

Bohemian

44 High Street

Hardly deserving of a separate listing is the brief use of the Empress Winter Gardens as a cinema. No attempt was made at a proper conversion as patrons sat in basket chairs at tables on the existing flat floor to watch the films, shown continuously from 3pm to 10pm. Teas were served during the intervals. The Bohemian may have only lasted a couple of weeks (the opening barely a week later of the nearby Super can hardly have helped) and it was certainly closed by the end of the year. The premises in later years became the Grange furniture shop and a branch of Next but are now a Wetherspoon's public house, The Moon Under Water.

Monday 21 February 1921

Super / Carlton

24 Clarendon Road

The Super was a conversion of a roller skating rink which did not provide the ideal shape for a cinema auditorium. A prominent London architect, F. Edward Jones, did everything possible. A proscenium arch and screen were erected across one corner and the stalls seats on a properly sloping floor were arranged to face it. A narrow upper viewing gallery was converted into a balcony with just two rows of seats that did not face the screen and the admission price was lower than for the stalls to reflect this shortcoming. The total

The Carlton Watford in 1973. The surviving Palace Theatre can be just seen to the right.

Interior views of the Carlton Watford after its 1963 reconstruction. Note the awkward V shape of the back wall and the supporting columns.

to show talking pictures – from Saturday 15 December 1928, although these were only shorts made by British Talking Pictures at Welwyn. Around September 1930 the Super changed its name to the Carlton. Plans dated 11 May 1936 for alterations by architect Cecil Masey show a projected capacity of 1,039 people in the stalls and 90 in the balcony.

The Rank Organisation took a thirty-year lease at £2,080 per annum from 14 July 1950. Rank's reason for leasing the Carlton when it had both the Odeon and Gaumont is obscure, especially as the company then sublet it. As an independent, it fared better than the Empire or Plaza, thanks to its central position and larger capacity, but it had no circuit releases to play except for ABC programmes in weeks when the Essoldo played Fox CinemaScope pictures in the 1950s.

Rank actively ran the Carlton from 30 April 1962. It was then closed on Saturday 20 July 1963 to be geared up as a replacement for the Odeon. The changes were substantial. The old ornate proscenium arch was removed; the small balcony was sealed off; false walls enclosed a new auditorium seating 778 and a cluster of lights was set in a new angular dome in the ceiling. Re-opening took place on 23 September 1963 with a two-week run of the period comedy hit *Tom Jones* (one of the stars, Diane Cilento, made a personal appearance) and the Odeon closed two months later.

The Carlton then shared with the Gaumont (which later took the Odeon name and was divided into three screens) the pick of the new releases, including those shown by the ABC circuit elsewhere. When EMI (which owned the ABC circuit) took over the Empire in 1976, it clearly intended the cinema to show the films booked by the ABC circuit. After it invested in twinning the Empire,

number of seats was 1,228. Wall panels were decorated in a Chinese tapestry design and the ceiling rose to a central dome from which hung an elaborate chandelier bearing white electric torches and a large illuminated globe. There was a tea lounge to the right-hand side of the stage and an orchestra numbering eight.

The opening attraction was *Kismet,* starring Otis Skinner, and the Super was for a time assured of consistently up-to-date programmes by being part of a group of sixty-five cinemas. It was the first Watford cinema

which could then play two ABC releases at a time, Rank no longer saw any point in operating the Carlton and surrendered the property to its owners on expiry of the lease on 19 July 1980. The Carlton's last programme was *Zombies – Dawn of the Dead* plus *The Great British Striptease* which ended its week's run on Saturday 12 July 1980, giving Rank a week to remove useful equipment and fittings. The Carlton was demolished in 1982 and its site is now occupied by an office block called Arliss Court and the Green Room Bar and Café that forms an extension of the adjacent Palace Theatre.

The Plaza Watford has been renamed the Odeon in early March 1937 but the original name is still used by the attached café. The car park entrance is at the end of the side road.

Monday 29 April 1929

Plaza / Odeon

125–7 The Parade, High Street
(corner of Albert Road)

With 2,060 seats, the Plaza had the largest seating capacity of any cinema auditorium ever built in Hertfordshire (very closely followed by the Gaumont Watford). It was a genuine super cinema of its time (architects: Emden, Egan and Co.) with a prominent dome above the corner entrance, an exceptionally spacious entrance foyer with mahogany panelling, a large café attached to the theatre,

The Odeon (ex-Plaza) Watford in early March 1937. The 2 manual/8 rank Compton organ remained until 1960.

and a well-proportioned auditorium with a sense of real spaciousness and luxury. The stage had a semi-circular front and a depth of 18ft to the footlights to enable stage shows to be presented, while there was an orchestra pit to accommodate twelve musicians and the console of the two-manual eight-rank Compton organ (some 2,000 pipes were located in two chambers to the left of the proscenium arch; they were capable of rendering almost every instrument in a symphony orchestra). There was also a car park for 250 vehicles. The Plaza opened at the end of the silent era and its first talkie was the Al Jolson smash hit, *The Singing Fool*, from Monday 8 July 1929.

In July 1936 the Odeon circuit announced that it had acquired the Plaza. In selling the cinema, its owners were undoubtedly influenced by the fact that Odeon had submitted plans for a new cinema a few doors along where the end of The Parade met St Albans Road (architects T. P. Bennett based the exterior design on their Haverstock Hill Odeon in north London; it provided for 1,527 seats). It was cheaper and quicker for Odeon to obtain the Plaza instead and the cinema changed hands on 28 September, being re-named the Odeon with effect from Monday 12 October. It then seated 1,253 in the stalls, 736 in the balcony. The organ console was re-located to a lift in the centre of the disused orchestra pit. (The organ was removed to Victoria Hall Evangelical Church, Wandsworth, in 1960.)

Both in size and location (in the county's largest town), the Plaza was an important takeover for the rapidly expanding Odeon circuit and it soon benefitted from the strong programmes that the circuit was able to obtain. It came under the same management as the town's Gaumont during the 1940s, then both became part of the Rank Organisation. In the early 1960s there were not enough good films to supply the two very large cinemas. Initially, the better programmes were generally assigned to the Odeon (the new "Rank release") but the more modern Gaumont must have seemed best suited to survive (besides which, Rank had the smaller Carlton) and the Odeon closed on Saturday 30 November 1963 after a week's run of *In the French Style* plus *The Girl in the Headlines*. It was demolished in February 1964 and replaced by an ugly new purple and grey brick structure accommodating a supermarket with corner entrance at ground-floor level (originally Cater's) and entertainment facilities above (originally the Top Rank Suite), entered to the left of the corner. The Top Rank Suite for dining and dancing maintained a Rank Organisation interest in the replacement building but the space was soon relinquished for nightclub use. In January 2002 the ground floor retail area was available for rent as the last occupant, Multiyork, had relocated elsewhere in the city centre, while the nightclub's current name was Destinys. An Iceland store at the rear occupied the former cinema car park.

Monday 3 May 1937

Gaumont / Odeon

65 The Parade, High Street

Built close to the Odeon, in a slightly more central position, the Gaumont was the only theatre in Hertfordshire directly associated with the giant Gaumont-British concern. (The Gaumonts at Barnet and St Albans were Odeon theatres renamed after the two circuits came under joint administration). This was a scheme taken over by a subsidiary, Gaumont Super Cinemas, from the entrepreneur Lou Morris who had acquired the site and commissioned his regular architects of the period, the Norwich practice of J. Owen Bond. (The same combination worked on a later scheme at North Watford which was sold to Odeon.) Gaumont Super Cinemas was a collaboration between Gaumont and the Hyams and Gale partnership that also reconstructed an old theatre into the Gaumont at Oldham, Lancashire, and built the largest of all English cinemas, the Gaumont State at Kilburn, north London.

According to the plans, the Gaumont Watford seated exactly 2,000: 1,398 in the stalls, 602 in the circle. Set back from the adjacent shops, the front was particularly dull, perhaps because the planners reduced the height to conform to the other buildings. The cinema entrance was in the centre with a shop to the left and the entrance to the first-floor restaurant to the right. The central

The Gaumont Watford in 1963. (See also front cover.)

Auditorium of the Odeon (ex-Gaumont) Watford, taken 2 June 1983. (From a colour transparency by Allen Eyles.)

One of the mini-cinemas under the balcony of the Odeon (ex-Gaumont) Watford, 2 June 1983. (From a colour transparency by Allen Eyles.)

windows above the entrance were part of the restaurant while the upper walls to each side were designed for two largish posters advertising the cinema's programmes.

The auditorium was very simple in design, with three bands of concealed lighting across the front ceiling and down the side walls. Whereas the splay walls of cinemas normally carried pierced decorative friezes or panels to hide the openings for ventilation and the organ chamber, here they were presented, simply and unadorned, as a honeycomb-like pattern of circular holes on the side walls. For stark modernity, the auditorium was matched only by the similar treatment of the splay walls at the later Odeon Camberwell, south London, although various Odeons had experimented with more discreet vents in the same manner. The organ was a three-manual eight-rank Wurlitzer which was often heard on radio broadcasts by resident organist Tommy Dando.

Guest of honour at the opening was Will Hay, the comedian whose film *Good Morning, Boys!* was part of the first show.

During the war, Arthur Courtney was organist and also general manager. He staged organ interludes whenever the films left enough time, usually playing for around fifteen minutes, with the audience humming to old favourites as their titles were announced on the screen and slides of appropriate scenes shown. After the war, the Wurlitzer was rarely heard. A fire broke out in the early hours of Monday 31 December 1956, destroying the CinemaScope screen (installed in November 1954), organ console and piano. Only the screen was replaced (by the evening of the same day). The rest of the organ was removed to the Methodist Church, Biggleswade, around 1959. The cinema now had 1,948 seats.

In the early 1960s, bingo was tried on Sunday afternoons. There were one-night live shows featuring stars such as Nina and Frederick, Count Basie and his Orchestra, the Dave Brubeck Quartet, John Leyton and Cliff Richard. After the Odeon had been closed for nearly a year, the Gaumont took over its name from 20 September 1964. The new Odeon performed well enough to warrant a 'drop wall conversion' by which the rear stalls became two mini-cinemas, side by side. In this case, reputedly because the circuit's managing director of that time lived locally, Odeons 2 and 3 were outfitted to a higher standard (with carpeted side walls) than triples elsewhere. The conversion took place without the cinema closing. It became a three-screen 'Film Centre' from 2 June 1974 when Woody Allen's *Sleeper* played in 612-seat Odeon 1 (the old circle, using the existing screen), *Busting* plus *I Escaped From Devil's Island* occupied the 120-seat Odeon 2 and *The Dove* was the attraction in 120-seat Odeon 3. The entire front stalls area was disused.

In 1983, Rank entered into negotiations to sell the Odeon – such a colossal sum was apparently offered that Rank found it too hard to refuse. Cinema attendances nationally were in steady decline but, nevertheless, abandoning a cinema in good shape in as important a town as Watford indicated that the Rank Organisation was not as fully committed to film exhibition as it had been. There was no talk of any replacement cinemas on part of the site. The Odeon closed on Saturday 15 October 1983 with *War Games* in Odeon 1, *Heat and Dust* in Odeon 2, and *Young Warriors* in Odeon 3. The wide auditorium section was demolished first, in November-December 1983, and has since been occupied by the rear end of Sainsbury's supermarket and an access road (called Gaumont Approach) to loading bays plus a multi-storey car park. The entrance block came down in January 1984, to be replaced by a new building with its frontage further forward, in line with the adjacent shops to which it is directly attached. In early 2002, the HFC Bank, Leeds Building Society and Holland and Barrett fill the space where the Gaumont stood while the site's entertainment tradition is upheld, in a rather different style, by Riley's first-floor pool room.

Saturday 27 November 1937

Odeon

405 St Albans Road, North Watford

There was keen interest in providing the rapidly increasing residential population of North Watford with a cinema. Early in 1936 architects J. Owen Bond submitted plans for a Ritz cinema in St Albans Road and the licensing authority gave permission to proceed on 19 February. As in the case of the Gaumont, the promoter was Lou Morris who registered the company Ritz (Watford) Ltd on 8 August 1936. Another prominent cinema architect and entrepreneur, Major W. J. King (who had built the Ritz Potters Bar), proposed a cinema on the corner of St Albans Road and the Watford By-Pass (on the north side of the present Dome Roundabout) and one set of 1936 plans named this as an Odeon.

Work began on the Ritz in spring 1937. Lou Morris made a habit of selling his cinemas, usually during construction or shortly after opening. In this case, while the Ritz was still being built, Morris sold it to Odeon and so it opened as the Odeon North Watford, about a mile away from the town centre Odeon. The circuit did not believe in cinema organs and cancelled the one that had been planned, although pipe chambers had been provided under the stage. The Odeon was built for a contract figure of around £32,000 and outfitting cost a further £6,936 3s 7d. The opening attraction was the British-made *Wings of the Morning* in early Technicolor with Henry Fonda.

The wide frontage was in red brick, built high enough to obscure the pitched roof of the auditorium from the street in front. It had red and green neon and five tall windows fronting the circle lounge. This was very presentable but gave no clue to the

The Odeon North Watford in November 1937. The entrance to the car park is at the back of the cinema.

The striking foyer of the Odeon North Watford in 1937.

bold decorative scheme within, devised by leading specialists Mollo and Egan (whose work also graced the Embassy Waltham Cross opened nine days earlier). Gold and silver colours were used throughout, relieved in the auditorium by green Odeon carpet and upholstery. The entrance hall and circle lounge were strikingly designed with a stylised "orchard panel" upstairs.

The auditorium seated 1,394: 942 in the stalls, 452 in the circle. It was even more imaginative with its concealed lighting in bands across the ceiling and the 'cut away' treatment of the side walls – making it the most impressive place to see films in Watford and one of the few outstanding examples of 1930s cinema design in Hertfordshire.

Unfortunately, the Odeon was not allowed to do as well as it might. Its suburban location dictated that it played second run to the cinemas in the centre of Watford,

The splendid interior of the Odeon North Watford, seen in 1937 with its colourful screen curtains on display.

showing the same films weeks after them and losing much of the potential audience. Although its situation was not as dire as that of the Odeon Rickmansworth, which had closed in early 1957, it became one of fourteen Odeons and Gaumonts put up for auction on 22 April 1959 even though it was still open. An acceptable bid was received and it closed on Saturday 30 May 1959 with the British comedy *Carlton-Browne of the F.O.* supported by *Girl in the Picture*, a programme which had played the town centre Odeon from 3 to 9 May. For manager Owen S. Bishop, it was a sad end to nineteen years of running the cinema.

The Odeon was converted into a Waitrose supermarket. Its frontage remained little altered although the stone parapet had become rather discoloured by the mid-1980s. The circle foyer survived as supermarket offices but the decorative panels had been painted over and a false ceiling inserted. Above the storeroom in the former balcony, the plasterwork of the auditorium ceiling and upper side walls was still in place. The arrival of a new Asda supermarket nearby brought an end to the building's second lease of life in October 1987 and it was demolished in January 1989. It has been replaced by the thirty-one flats of Gladesmere Court at the front of the site with gardens at the rear.

The circle lounge of the Odeon North Watford in 1937 with vivid decoration by Eugene Mollo and the standard Odeon circuit style of carpet and upright ashstands.

Friday 19 January 1996

Warner / Warner Village

Woodside Leisure Park,
North Orbital Road, Garston

The Woodside Leisure Park was a smaller development than most of its type, alongside the A405 on an 8.5 acre site more than two miles north of the town centre. Its proximity to the M1 meant that it could potentially attract patrons from a very wide area as well as the residents of Watford itself.

The use of the Council-owned site was a subject of much controversy, according to the 1996 *Book of Watford II* by J.B. Nunn. This was originally the site of the Woodside sports fields and complex opened in 1955 by the Duke of Edinburgh and in 1958 a deed of covenant was entered that the land could be used only as public playing fields. However, as an infill site with poor drainage, it was ill-suited for football and cricket and was leased out for twenty-one years to become a golf range. More than a year before the lease expired in 1988, the Council was envisaging a six-screen cinema and ice rink on the site and a developer, Citygrove, proposed a 'City Dome' leisure park that was much criticised for its dome-shaped appearance and content (which included a nightclub). A public inquiry was held in 1991.

The Warner Village multiplex at Garston in 2002. Originally the famous Warner Bros WB shield logo was mounted on the glass of the gabled entrance and was more impressive than the present signage which displays the trademark in much more modest form along with that of co-owner Village Roadshow. (Photograph by Allen Eyles.)

The scheme went ahead without a dome, built by Watford Leisure, an associated company of Citygrove. The £10 million project originally made provision for an eight-screen cinema, a ten-pin bowling alley, ice skating rink, child-care area, two restaurants, lounge with bar and parking space for 835 cars. The cinema occupied nearly half the area that was built on. The ice rink was dropped.

There was intense competition for the cinema space from Warner Bros and from Odeon which, having sold its three-screen cinema in 1983, now decided that it wanted to be back in Watford again. Both chains thought they had secured the site and announced it as part of their multiplex programme but Warner Bros finally clinched the deal. There were free screenings on the weekend of 13 and 14 January 1996 but the complex officially opened on the following Friday, the same day as the Warner off Purley Way, Croydon, which also had eight screens.

Its modern facilities and lively ambience proved an immediate attraction to the younger audience and forced the closure of the town's last traditional cinema, the ABC, on 26 September 1996. There was now no cinema anywhere near the city centre.

The Warner has become the Warner Village, reflecting a partnership arrangement with the Australian circuit, Village Roadshow, rather than any claim to a village-like setting. The multiplex seats in total slightly more than the Gaumont and slightly less than the Plaza when these two town-centre cinemas opened in the 1930s. But, of course, the big difference is that its 2,026 seats are spread across eight different auditoria as follows: 249, 233, 264, 330, 221, 208, 215 and 306. The eight screens offer more choice at any one time than Watford cinemagoers had in the past, but now most films have extended runs instead of only a week or less as was the case in the distant past.

The box office is outside in the open air. As in most multiplexes, there is a huge, lofty foyer. The upper area is largely painted black to conceal the corrugated roof and air ducts. There is a curving bank of video screens suspended on a frame along with Warner Bros cartoon figures like Bugs Bunny and Elmer Fudd, paralleled by wavy lines of flashing blue and yellow V shapes in neon or fibre optic. The Warner Bros shield logo is projected in motion across the blue carpet. A games room is on one side and the ice-cream counter and confectionery pic'n'mix on the other with the counter for popcorn and drinks at the back. A corridor leads to the eight screens, four to each side, their numbers announced in large pink illuminated signs.

WELWYN

Friday 29 July 1938

Pavilion

London Road

With 801 seats on a single floor, the Pavilion was built in under three months to plans by J. Edmund Farrell which had originally been prepared for a site in Cheshunt. It was set back lengthways along the London Road with a car park and cycle shelter (both very helpful for this location), and even a café. The presentation on the

The Welwyn Pavilion in October 1961. (Photograph by H. J. Stull.)

opening Friday was the MGM musical *Rosalie*, with Eleanor Powell and Nelson Eddy. In later years the Pavilion rather mysteriously became, for a while, one of only two "miscellaneous theatres" in the list of cinemas administered by Circuits Management Association, a company formed in 1948 to run the huge Odeon and Gaumont circuits.

Despite a somewhat isolated position well outside the town, the Pavilion lasted well enough until the severe attendance decline of the late 1950s. In June 1961 it was sold to P. Tabor for conversion into a motor vehicle distribution centre and a wave of controversy was unleashed. There were two public meetings of protest and 6,000 people signed a petition against the change of use. P. Tabor indicated that they would release the building for continued cinema use if another site could be found for their purposes, and the last owners of the Pavilion declared that they would take a twenty-one

year lease if a suitable building for a new cinema was provided. Welwyn Rural Council's housing and town planning committee narrowly recommended plans be drawn up for a cinema on the eastern side of Prospect Place but the Council as a whole rejected this because a new civic centre was envisaged for the site and there was not enough space for a cinema as well.

The Pavilion stayed open for a while. An advertisement in the local press for the Kirk Douglas western *The Last Sunset* in October 1961 added: "Just to indicate we haven't closed – yet". The November monthly programme cruelly altered the regular slogan "Your week is not complete without a visit to the Pavilion" to read "Your week is not complete without a visit to the petrol pumps". Closure was set for 1 January 1962 after the Christmas holidays, then abruptly advanced to Saturday 2 December 1961 after a six-day run of the Dirk Bogarde drama *Victim* plus *Attempt to Kill*. Fittings were removed in December and it was converted to Acland and Tabor's car distribution centre in January 1962. By 1985, it had become the vehicle testing part of Godfrey Davis (Welwyn) Ltd, while the old café was a car wash. Additions and alterations had rendered it virtually unrecognisable. In 2002, it remains in use by Godfrey Davis and the truncated upper frontage can be detected behind the slightly lower reception area built on front. The original auditorium has long gone but the side walls of the large garage may have been part of the old cinema.

WELWYN GARDEN CITY

Saturday 11 October 1924

Kinema

Parkway Hall

The opening night show was *The Net* plus *Sentinels of the Sea* and Gaumont Graphic (newsreel). This cinema in the Parkway Hall operated two nights a week at first with adult prices at 8d, 1/3d, and 1/6d. Seats were reservable for an additional 3d. There was a "Bijou Orchestra" to accompany the silent films. It was soon opening six nights a week but by April 1925 film shows were on Tuesdays and Saturdays only. Later the number of days varied according to other events such as amateur stage shows. The Kinema, sited next to the former Welwyn Department Store, closed in 1928 when the new Theatre opened.

The Kinema at Parkway Hall circa 1925. (Courtesy of H. J. Stull.)

Friday 27 January 1928

Welwyn Theatre / Embassy

Parkway

Seating 1,100 the Welwyn Theatre was a bold venture at a time when the Garden City's population was only 6,000. It was a gesture of confidence in the future but also an amenity that would actively encourage new residents to settle in the area. Designed for use as both a cinema and a theatre, it was not expected to start repaying its

The Welwyn Theatre, circa 1928.

The original interior of the Welwyn Theatre in 1928. Note the reflective plates on the side wall,

investors for several years and it had to be built with economic constraints. The result was still an auditorium of striking character that attracted considerable attention in architectural circles including a six-page illustrated article, "New Wine: The Theatre at Welwyn" by Ronald Orfeur in the *Architectural Review*, April 1928. Three illustrations appeared in the highly influential 1930 book, *Modern Theatres and Cinemas*, by P. Morton Shand.

A link to the new Welwyn film studios was envisaged by which the new cinema might be used for private screenings in the afternoons and for sneak previews of locally-made productions in the evenings. Whether this ever happened is not known.

The Garden City's architect, Louis de Soissons, collaborated on the Theatre with Arthur W. Kenyon (whose later work as a cinema architect included the notable Palace Chatham). The site gives the impression that it was a little out of the way, not facing into the main shopping area although certainly part of it. The main façade was in a very formal Georgian style to fit in with the predetermined look of the new town. Most of the first floor and the whole of the second floor at the front were given over to offices and the building looked remarkably restrained and unostentatious for a cinema, which was its primary function. The square foyer was reached through three sets of doors emphasised only by stone surrounds on the frontage. A neon sign in tasteful italic announced "The Welwyn Theatre" between the two rows of windows. The foyer was an open area with a Chinese-style light fitting over the centre and a small theatrical-style paybox window in a side wall. Doors at the back led to the stalls floor while a staircase on the right led off to the small balcony.

The auditorium had a rectangular shape

with a low ceiling in order to save costs. The sloping stalls floor had 930 seats in straight rows. There were 170 seats in five straight rows in the balcony which extended only over the rear passage of the stalls. The design strikingly prefigures the low-ceilinged semi-stadium cinemas of the 1930s. The walls were covered in moulded wooden panels with, on each side, three vertical panels containing small rectangular pieces of frosted glass. The wide proscenium arch was edged with Chinese shapes and the ornamental brackets where the main walls joined the splay walls also looked Chinese in inspiration.

The Welwyn Theatre with its re-designed foyer in 1936.

The building was fully equipped for live theatrical use but the depth of the stage was restricted to 29ft to save money. Nevertheless, there was a full grid, a sectional stage floor, four sets of curtains on counterweights, a full electrical light installation and four small dressing rooms. The Theatre was carefully designed for good acoustics to overcome its rectangular shape which placed the furthest seats 100ft from the curtain. The orchestra pit could be covered over to extend the stage in an apron.

The opening night presentation was the German film of *Faust*. A week later, on the Thursday and Friday, the specially-formed Welwyn Repertory Company put on a three-act comedy by a local author, *When the Heart is Young*. Until sound came in, films were accompanied by music on a gramophone system, the panatrope, using loudspeakers behind perforated panels on the splay walls, although originally the Theatre had its own resident orchestra under the direction of Bromley Derry. In November 1928 the London Grand Opera Company presented *Cavalleria Rusticana* and *Carmen* on successive nights. From 1929-73 (except for the war years and 1963) the Welwyn Drama Festival was staged here and in the

Part of the redesigned auditorium of the Welwyn Theatre in 1936.

The Welwyn Theatre as the Embassy in June 1983. (Photograph by H. J. Stull.)

early 1930s annual pantomimes were established.

In April 1936 the Theatre was acquired by one of the many rapidly-expanding cinema circuits of the period, Shipman and King. The new owners immediately carried out substantial alterations. A modern paybox and new light fitting in a 10ft diameter saucer dome were introduced in the foyer, relegating the old ticket window to a chocolate kiosk. The wood panelling of the auditorium was painted over and the glass panels (which had a distracting effect of reflecting light) were scrapped in favour of stencilled decorations with a nature theme. Floral patterns in fibrous plaster covered all the grilles while the decoration around the proscenium arch was replaced by straight bands in fibrous plaster. The decorative consultant was Louis Ososki and the result was more in keeping with the 1930s, pleasant but less distinctive. Later in the 1930s, S & K contemplated building a second cinema in the town, to match the pairs they had elsewhere, and plans were drawn up by architect David E. Nye but the proposed site does not seem to have been publicly announced.

The Theatre's stage continued to be used – the Welwyn Thalians presented *The Dancing Years* in 1960. Local resident Harry Stull has noted: "A fire engulfed the stage area on the night of 27 November 1962 after the opening performance of *Carousel* by the Welwyn Thalians. The rebuilding work included the complete reconstruction of the stage and the installation of the most up-to-date remote-control lighting equipment. At its re-opening in 1963, the building was renamed Embassy." Embassy was the name long favoured by S & K for its leading cinemas. The Thalians returned with a live production of *South Pacific* in 1964.

The first threat to the cinema's continued existence came in 1981 when EMI (which now owned S & K) applied for a bingo licence as "a safeguard". When the same company closed the County at Hertford in 1982, it was thought that the Embassy would then be twinned and kept going but in 1983 it was sold and closed on Saturday 6 August with the final showing of *The Dark Crystal*. Over the years since its 1936 modernisation it had changed little – as at the Hertford County, only the entrance hall had been updated, although it had been re-seated at least twice and in its final years seated just over 1,000.

It is amazing how little fuss seems to have been caused by the closure of the town's only mainstream cinema with its valuable theatrical facilities. After having been set on fire, the building was demolished in great haste to make way for a £2 million office block. The new building, called Charter House, opened in spring 1986 with a front elevation that is almost identical to that of the old cinema to blend in with the adjacent buildings, and is occupied by the East and North Hertfordshire Health Authority. A plaque on the wall to the left of the entrance, erected during the national Centenary of Cinema celebrations in 1996, recalls the former building on the site.

Opened on 8 December 1973 by a local resident, Dame Flora Robson, Welwyn's Council-owned Campus West Theatre was functioning as a part-time art house cinema before the Embassy closed. It began screening some mainstream films from July 1989 with *Indiana Jones and the Last Crusade.*

One of its projectionists, Steve Baker, notes: "The public areas that are reached via a sweeping curved stairway house a flourishing art gallery and ample theatre bar (15m x 30m). The decor is predominantly deep red and white. The ceiling has a shallow, stepped, curve. On entering the double doors, the theatre is accessed via passages containing stills and gold-framed poster quads, with the floor gently sloping upwards to the rear of the stadium-design auditorium. The plain brick walls are painted in 'midnight blue' and the theatre tabs are deep red. The seating is of dark blue colour. The screen is flown for live events. There is a large orchestra pit. The cinema is very well used and has undergone a comprehensive improvement and refurbishment programme over recent years. These include full access for wheelchair users and modern air conditioning. There are five large dressing rooms and a fly tower with thirteen lines recently upgraded to hemps.

"A large 'theatrical design' poster and stills board from the exterior of the Embassy Cinema is affixed in the bar and used to publicise forthcoming attractions. There is vertical ribbing in gold and shallow black spaces for pictures and stills. Also, there is a Simplex E7 projector restored and a première spot lantern on display from the former Curzon Cinema in Hatfield."

In 2002 the Campus West Theatre shows films predominantly, ranging from art house films to the better mainstream attractions, but also includes a busy live schedule of professional and amateur performances. It seats 326.

BIBLIOGRAPHY

ARTICLES

Hitchin
"The Picturedrome: Hitchin's first cinema" by Arthur L. Codling, *Hertfordshire Countryside*, August 1972.
"Sixty years of the silver screen in Hitchin" by Pat Gadd, *Hertfordshire Countryside*, October 1979.

Letchworth
"The oldest purpose-built cinema?" [Letchworth Palace] by Audrey Wadowska, *Hertfordshire Countryside*, July 1970.

Rickmansworth
"The Era of the Cinema in Rickmansworth" by E.V. Parrott, *Rickmansworth Historian*, Autumn 1964 and Autumn 1965.

Sawbridgeworth
"The Cinema That Lost Its Name" by Dorothy Cleal, *Hertfordshire Countryside*, March 2002, pages 32 & 33.

St Albans
"The Alpha Picture Palace, St Albans" by Audrey Wadowska. *Cinema Theatre Association Bulletin*, No 2, April 1967, pages 2 & 3.

Standon
"A Trip to the Pictures" by Dorothy Cleal, *Hertfordshire Countryside*, August 1998.

Watford
"Watford's Edwardian Entertainment" by George Lorimer, Hertfordshire Countryside, circa 1982.
"Watford Cinemas past and present" by Chris Clegg and Ivor Buckingham, *Hertfordshire Countryside*, November and December 1975, February 1976.

BOOKS

The Beginnings of the Cinema in England, Vol. 1: 1894-1896. By John Barnes. University of Exeter Press, 1998.
The Granada Theatres. By Allen Eyles. Cinema Theatre Association/BFI Publishing, 1998.
A Last Complete Performance – Watford's cinema history in focus. By Ivor Buckingham, 1989.

Readers interested in cinemas generally should consider joining the Cinema Theatre Association, established in 1967 to promote serious interest in all aspects of cinema buildings. Its bi-monthly *Bulletin* will provide an up-date on Hertfordshire developments and it also publishes an illustrated magazine, *Picture House*. Subscriptions (£15 annually in August 2002) and further information (enclose s.a.e) are available from the Membership Secretary, Neville C. Taylor, Flat One, 128 Gloucester Terrace, London W2 6HP.

INDEX

Page numbers in **bold type** indicate the principal
reference to Hertfordshire cinemas
   Only films whose screening was of particular
local significance are listed